Enlightenment for Nitwits

THE COMPLETE GUIDE TO 2012 & BEYOND!

Shepherd Hoodwin

Summerjoy Press

LAGUNA NIGUEL, CALIFORNIA

2011

ENLIGHTENMENT FOR NITWITS
The Complete Guide to 2012 & Beyond!

Summerjoy Press
99 Pearl
Laguna Niguel CA 92677-4818
http://summerjoy.com
publishing@summerjoy.com

http://enlightenmentfornitwits.com
Twitter: @EnlightenNitwit, @shepherdh
https://www.facebook.com/EnlightenmentforNitwits

Printed in the U.S.A.
ISBN 978-1-885469-12-0
Library of Congress Control Number: 2011902344

Members of Congress: *I expect you to read this. There's no excuse—it's in your library. No, having your aides read it is not good enough.*

Jacket design and photo illustration are by Melody V. Cassen.
Interior design is by Shepherd Hoodwin.

Cover art **images** are from Dreamstime and iStockphoto. The Summerjoy Press logo is from a painting by Kathy Anderson. The author photo is by the author. Most interior photos are from iStockphoto and Shutterstock. The photo of the Dalai Lama is courtesy of Kechara. Photos of Freud, Amun-Ra, Khajuraho, hundred-year-old woman, Confucius, crop circle, and "Jesus at 33" were found on the Internet, and we were unable to determine the owners; if you hold the copyright to one of them, please contact us. **Quotes** from God, Satan, and the Buddha were obtained with the generous assistance of the original Creative Artists Agency.

Dedication

Lyn Wilde Oberlink

My honorary mother

An angel who showed me my path, believed in me,
and is still the best second banana in the business.

Acknowledgments

I could never have written this book
without the Universe, who made it all possible.
I'd also like to thank my spirit guide, Fred;
my agent, Max; and the members of the Academy.

Important Announcement
from the
MAYAN CALENDAR COMMITTEE

Due to circumstances beyond our control, 2012 has been postponed. Therefore, the order of years shall be as follows:

2011
2013
2014
2015
2016
2012
2017

We are working with the Vatican to correct the Gregorian civil calendar as soon as possible.

Additional alterations may be required due to unexpected sunspots, meteorites, or Supreme Court appointments. To stay apprised of further 2012 developments, sign up for our free newsletter at http://www.MayanCalendarCommittee.org. You may also receive occasional emails from our specially chosen marketing partners, such as the Great Black White & Red All Over Brotherhood, Ascended Masters"R"Us, and Ayahuasca N' Stuff.

If you already registered for the Crystalline Ascension, your deposit will be automatically applied to the new December 21, 2012. However, if you wish, you can request a refund at refund@MayanCalendar

Committee.org. Be sure to include your full birth information and your spiritual name. If you want to check first to see whether you'll still be alive in 2012, contact us at death@MayanCalendarCommittee.org. If you are concerned about passing the time until 2012 arrives, there are some adorable kitten and puppy videos on YouTube.

We apologize for any inconvenience.

We have received a number of inquiries as to whether 2012 will be the dawn of a new age of enlightenment and bliss, or the end of life as we know it. All signs clearly point to one answer: yes and no.

For more information on how 2012 can benefit you or your company, please visit us at http://www.MayanCalendarCommittee.org.

Quezaltepeque Hoodwin, Chairman
The Association of Shamans &
Soothsayers (ASS),
Mayan Calendar Committee

CONTENTS

BUT SERIOUSLY, FOLKS

I have written this book for the joy of it, in the hope it will bring joy to others, with love and respect for everyone's path as well as for the awesome goofiness of being.

In real life, I am an intuitive, channel, and author of serious metaphysical books. Spirituality is central to my life. I am also gay and Jewish, but I won't try to convert you unless you really want me to.

We each have unique beliefs and sensibilities. Even the most good-natured humor can sometimes offend people, especially on topics like religion and politics. As much as I have tried to avoid that, I know we all want to be heard, so feedback can be sent to deaththreats@ enlightenmentfornitwits.com. I promise that each and every email will be followed up by the appropriate authorities.

However, great wisdom teachers love to laugh. They see the absurdities of life and self, and generally don't mind jokes about their religions. I was told that among psychics, Jesus is known for his dry sense of humor—no kidding. And a recent survey showed that 92% of Jewish mothers like Jewish mother jokes as long as you eat.

This book is mostly a collection of pieces on a wide range of themes that I wrote over the years to share with friends and online groups. When someone suggested a book, I came up with enlightenment as a unifying theme. I don't regard myself as enlightened, whatever that might prove to mean, but working toward it is a worthy goal. As to my being a sex symbol—fifty million Frenchmen can't be wrong.

WHY THIS IS NOT A WEIRD BOOK

This is not a weird book. I know you know this, because you wouldn't have bought it if you thought it was weird. At least, I hope you bought it. After all, you're a divine being: you *deserve* to own this book. Owning it in either electronic or paper form is an important statement to the Universe that you are ready to receive abundance.

But the point is that you're reading this book, and you don't read weird books, although you know people who do, like those fundies who read about how they're going to rapturously disappear into Heaven while the Ford Taurus they were driving crashes through the window of Big Lots and everybody else has to duke it out with sexy but demonic talk show hosts.

I am not a professional guru; I am a real person, just like you. I enjoy mayonnaise jello rolls and shootin' small animals from helicopters just as much as the next average person. At the same time, I am a seeker who cares deeply about the future of humanity (d*rn that global warming). In my spare time, when I'm not busy smoking medical marijuana or having carrot juice enemas, I channel Doreen, a former Lemurian high priestess.[1] "But isn't channeling weird?" you're thinking (I know this because I am a gifted psychic). Not at all.

---

[1] She's now retired, but keeps busy with gardening and volunteer work.

People have been doing it throughout history—it's as normal as alien abductions.

As we approach December 21, 2012, the end of the Mayan calendar, we naturally think about things like getting a new calendar, and preparing for what's ahead. 2012 is an unprecedented opportunity for transformation, and enlightenment is about to become the next big thing. It's not going to be enough anymore to have an iPad. You won't get into the hottest new clubs unless you can transcend space and time. Don't be left out! Put enlightenment at the top of your list, or when the jocks and cheerleaders ascend, you might be stuck in a parallel universe with the Chess Club. As the Mayan Calendar Committee says, "2012—It's Not Just for Wackos Anymore."

Before this groundbreaking guide was published, achieving enlightenment was an arduous task—it took years of meditation and study. However, working on yourself is the old-fashioned way of getting ahead spiritually, an outmoded paradigm.[2] This book will show you how to start at the top, without any of that messy self-examination.

Shepherd Hoodwin
Laguna Niguel, California
August 30, 2011
(Actually, I wrote this in 2004.)

---

[2] A paradigm is two dimes, or twenty cents.

HOW TO USE THIS BOOK

The Buddha taught that to become enlightened and attain nirvana, you must find nothingness. And if you're looking for nothingness, you came to the right place. This book gives you plenty of nothingness.

In fact, everything's here: all the nothingness you could hope for in one easy-to-read volume. As the title says, this is your *Complete Guide*. Absolutely nothing has been left in—that's how complete it is.

Okay, maybe it's not quite that complete—we're talking infinity and eternity here. Would you want to lug that much nothingness to the beach? If it were taken too far, you might be looking at a black hole, which can be a big mess. However, if I had called it *Enlightenment for Nitwits: The Incomplete Guide to 2012 & Beyond!*, would you have bought it? I didn't think so. In any case, it's complete enough for all normal enlightenment purposes. If you're not in absolute bliss by the end of it, you might want to increase your meds.

While we're on the subject of the title, some have asked me why I called it *Enlightenment for* Nitwits. The main reason is that *Dummies* and *Idiots* were trademarked (by the Bush administration, in 2001). These titles don't imply any disrespect for readers. In fact, I've been privileged to meet many of my readers, and they are among the most intelligent, caring, and good-smelling people I've ever run across. Such titles simply telegraph to potential buyers that the subject will be covered in an easily accessible manner. Isn't that what we're all looking for? With enlightenment, who wants to wade through long, arcane texts, in many cases written by people who didn't even bother to learn English! and then have to sit on the dirty floor of a drafty cave for forty years trying to figure it all out? I've already done the hard work so that you don't have to. This book, a combination of laughter yoga and colonic therapy, is Mr. Clean for the soul—it takes the drudgery out of spiritual growth. Every seeker will want to keep a copy next to his toilet.

Please note that this timeless book works whether you're preparing for 2012, or using it in any other year in the future or past (for example, if you're a time traveler). The principles of enlightenment don't change. However, if you're reading this before the invention of the printing press, be advised that it is forbidden to interfere with the course of human history.

I'd like to begin with a quote from my good friend the Dalai Lama. He, of course, starred in the classic Broadway musical *Hello, Dalai!* It featured a chorus line of singing and dancing monks who levitated several feet off the ground while holding trays of rice, as Dalai descended a staircase wearing a glorious crimson robe and Louis Armstrong sang the title song. It was an unforgettable moment in the annals of spirituality. Until that time, few had realized that His Holiness had such great legs.

One day, Dalai and I were sitting together in deep meditation. Suddenly, he said to me, "My son,"—that's what he calls me; we're not related—"My son, enlightenment is easy. Comedy is hard." And it's true. He's a great guy and I love him, but he really isn't that funny. It was then that he asked me to write this book, which is the fulfillment of an ancient prophesy first brought to light again when he discovered me at four years old doing stand-up on the playground. My test was to correctly identify the rubber chicken, fedora, and exploding cigar I had used in my previous lifetime as the Fifteenth Falai Lama. Of course, the true Falai Lama would know his own rubber chicken anywhere (mine is unusual in that it makes a farting sound as it shoots rubber eggs).

This book is easy to use. As you read the stories of my spiritual journey, simply be aware of your breath and feel gratitude welling up from deep within you that you're not me.

As a savvy humor consumer, you are no doubt aware that metaphysical comedy is a huge, brutally competitive field. However, I have managed to carve out a niche for myself and am well known for it worldwide among the 113 or so readers of my previous books. I hope that, with this book, I can reach an even larger audience, changing many people's lives, some of them for the better.

PART I

SELF-HELP
&
PERSONAL GROWTH

Chapter One shows you how to have a good attitude, which is the initial step to enlightenment.

Chapter 1

Inspiration for Today

LIFE'S GIFTS

Wise spiritual thinkers teach us that everything in life is a gift, often with hidden blessings or lessons.

For example, being hit by a bus might give you the insurance money to have the nose job you've always wanted. Without your venereal disease, you might not have met that cute doctor. If you hadn't been fired, you may never have become homeless and learned how to make dumpster art. We should not judge life's gifts.

Some of life's gifts come in beautiful packages; others, not so much. Some gifts are the wrong size, clash with everything we own, or are in icky taste. Some, we regift to our mother-in-law, who happens to like black velvet animal portraits and plastic figurines of Jesus on the Cross that squirt fake blood. Some, we throw in the back of our closet, where they stay until we die and our children find them, wondering, *What the h*ck[1] is that?* But they are all gifts.

My grandmother Hoodwin loved giving gifts and meticulously wrapped them. Once, many years ago, she

---

[1] Please note that there are no swear words in this book. According to the American Swearing Society (ASS), "Replacing a vowel with an asterisk in a four-letter word makes it a three-letter word plus a typographical symbol, suitable for the whole family." Since I am a spiritual person and never swear, I also use asterisks when speaking.

had a doctor's appointment in Chicago, and was instructed to bring specimens (both kinds). She was embarrassed to bring them on the train, so she wrapped them in beautiful paper and ribbons. Unfortunately, she left them on the luggage rack. No doubt someone found those packages and opened them. One hopes he realized that they were gifts, despite being feces and urine. Yes, we cannot judge life's gifts. Who knows what they had to teach him? Whatever it was, it was probably something he never forgot.

Sometimes we meet people who have beautiful wrapping but are full of cr*p, like my grandmother's package. Perhaps they teach us lessons about not wasting our time with a-holes. Sometimes we meet people who are not wrapped beautifully but are still a-holes. Regardless of the wrapping, they are part of life's gifts.

Sometimes gifts aren't wrapped at all, but are covered with tissue paper and placed in reusable "gift bags." Others are wrapped in the Sunday color comics. Just toss them in the trash. Those who give them are cheap and/or lazy tree-huggers. Surely a gift is worth a tree or two. On the other hand, keep gift cards—you can get cash for them.

Regardless, gifts that go straight to the trash are still gifts, just as movies that go straight to DVD are still movies, even though they are probably lousy. Cherish them all, for without them, you would not be who you are today. And remember: you are one of life's gifts to others—try to stay out of the garbage.

Now that you have a good attitude,
let's delve into how to focus your thoughts
so you can get everything you want.

Chapter 2

THE SECRET

I was thrilled to learn about *The Secret* on Oprah. As you probably know, *The Secret* teaches you how to harness the power of your mind to make your dreams come true.

I knew that what I really wanted was Brad Pitt. Using the methods of *The Secret*, I focused my thoughts on Brad Pitt falling in love with me. My spiritual guides told me that he was very close to calling and asking if he could move in with me. I didn't know what the Universe planned to do with Angelina Jolie and their kids, but that was none of my business; I just kept holding positive thoughts.

Part of *The Secret's* secret is that you must not have any negative thoughts—not even one. Sadly, I blew it. My negative thought lasted only about thirty seconds, but it shot down my whole year of visualizations and affirmations. That thought was, "Maybe he doesn't like redheads." It was over—Brad moved on and there was nothing I could do about it.

However, I am happy to report that I have learned my lesson, and this time I'm sure it will work with Hugh Jackman. If God doesn't want me to have Hugh Jackman, tough. I'm going to have him anyway, because I deserve him. I create my own reality, d*rn it! I truly and *completely* believe that. If he doesn't like redheads, I'll *make* him—that's how powerful my thoughts are.

I should get going. I have three hours of affirmations to do before bed.

AN UPDATE: I trust that you're getting everything you want, too. Isn't it wonderful to finally have it all? My goodness, since *The Secret*, I don't know what to do with all the money pouring in—it's almost more than I can keep track of. And the nonstop sex with incredibly hot men. And the fame and worldwide acclaim. I don't know if I can take it anymore.

Oddly, Hugh Jackman isn't returning my calls. Neither is Hugh Grant. Or Hugh Dancy. Or Hugh Laurie. Or any other Hughs. I thought that Hugh create your own reality. But Brad called, so I can't complain too much.

7

Sometimes you hit a pothole
on the road to enlightenment
because you had a bad childhood.
If that's the case, you might need therapy.

The following chapter isn't meant
to be a comprehensive survey
of therapeutic techniques,
which would be depressing.
However, it does provide a couple of points
to bear in mind when you look for someone to fix you.

Chapter 3

THERAPY

There's a sure test to determine whether you still have issues: Look down. If you see a body, you have issues. If you don't see a body, you *really* have issues.

In California, if you have a fear of intimacy, you can get a disabled parking permit. Ask your therapist about it today!

Now that we have therapy handled,
let's take a look at the ego,
because it's sure to come up in your therapy.

The main thing to remember
is that your ego is evil
and you need to destroy it,
like dandelions in the perfect yard of Self.
So get out your Weed-B-Gone and let's get going!

Chapter 4

EGO

I don't mean to brag, but I have *so* gotten rid of my ego.

I'm for peace and love, and can't stand bullies. I'd like to beat them all to a pulp.

Judgmental people are disgusting, too, don't you agree? They're so much worse than us good people who don't judge, they make me want to puke.

Therapy is about helping you cope with life,
which most therapists agree is a big pain in the *ss.
However, don't let that stop you from getting enlightened.
Just meditate upon the is-ness of what is.
This chapter shows you how.

Chapter 5

COPING

I f you can't find happiness in your own backyard, you never really lost it to begin with. I wish I had a backyard.

Next time you need a lift, stop at Starbucks and ask for a coffee enema.

"Suicide Hotline. How can we make your suicide more enjoyable today?"

IT'S A SMALL WORLD (AFTER ALL)

I visited Disney World in the 80s. At the time, most of the attractions consisted of riding in a little boat through a cave while things popped out at you and they played "It's a Small World (After All)" over and over. The lyrics are simple yet evocative: "It's a small world (after all). It's a small world (after all). It's a small world (after all). It's a small world (after all)." I swore after that short visit that if I ever heard the song again, I would commit a truly heinous crime, maybe including giving Mickey Mouse rat poison.

A year ago, I was telling a friend about this on the phone when I heard "It's a Small World (After All)" playing outside my window, presumably blaring from a truck. After that, I heard it at dinnertime about once a week. I figured that someone who lived in the complex drove it for work and it played whenever he parked. I had a neighbor who kept waking me at six a.m. with a work truck that beeped every time he backed up, as a safety precaution, and the beep could not be turned off. Now that I think about it, though, playing "It's a Small World (After All)" would be the opposite of a safety precaution, as it would attract children, who would then be run over.

I began to wonder if I was imagining it—maybe the song was just playing in my head. In any case, I realized that my intense hatred of "It's a Small World (After All)" was attracting to me the very thing I hated. I had to stop giving energy to "It's a Small World (After All)."

Recently, while taking a walk, I found the guilty vehicle—an ice cream truck. I had discounted that possibility because there aren't many children in this complex. Why would an ice cream truck come here? It was a huge, ancient white box. I felt compassion for the poor schmuck trying to make a living selling semi-dairy products one at a time, a seasonal business at best in this suburban area. The song actually sounded kind of cute up close, especially with the daffy boing between each line. When I read on Wikipedia that it is probably the most performed and translated song in the entire world, I felt compassion for the world, too. To my surprise, I didn't hate it anymore. All I can say is, it's a small world (after all).

A psychic told me that I have a large positive balance in my karmic bank account. However, the teller left to speak with a supervisor thirty-five years ago and never came back.

When it rains, it pours, and then it molds.

I was at Sears looking for a carry-on. I asked a young guy who worked there for directions, and he said (I swear), "The luggage department is on the lower level, but I don't know if they have suitcases."

While I was waiting for a flight, three different terrorists approached me and asked if I'd take some explosives for them in my carry-on luggage, but I said no. I didn't have room.

We are all one. Therefore, I am Barack Obama and Meryl Streep. I am also Dick Cheney and the Octo-mom. You win some, you lose some.

When I see shoppers with a baby in their shopping cart, I ask them what aisle they found it on.

HIGHER EDUCATION

Knowledge is one of our best tools for coping with the

physical plane. My grandmother Keller impressed upon me the importance of a college education. I had taken a year off after high school, and she somehow found out I had done that solely to aggravate her. She told me her story:

> When I was a girl in Warsaw, I studied with a college professor. He told me, "Irene, you study with me six months, and I'll have you in college." But then the war (WWI) broke out, so I didn't get a college education. Afterward, I came to this country, married your grandfather, and had your uncle and mother.
>
> When they got a little older, I studied with a college professor. He told me, "Irene, you study with me six months, and I'll have you in college." But then the war (WWII) broke out, and I had to help your grandfather in the store, so I didn't get a college education.
>
> But—I learned more from living than you could get from all the years of college education. I wouldn't trade what I learned from living for ten college educations. And what I learned from living is that you've got to have a college education.

So, inspired by my grandmother's wisdom, I got a college education, a B.M.[1] from U.O., and I'm so glad I did. I credit that with keeping me from having to get a job for five years.

---

[1] No, not one of those—a Bachelor of Music.

The Way requires you to relinquish all ambition and striving, so I've been working hard to be as lazy and unproductive as possible. Still, sometimes I fail, despite my best efforts, and revert to my old pattern of getting work done. However, I pick myself right up and get back on that recliner.

Do you remember pet rocks? Maybe, in reality, we're *their* pets—they live way longer than we do.

A CARD MY CAT WROTE

Dear Aunt Ethel,

I thought you'd like to see these pictures of me holding my pet person Shepherd. Doesn't he look fat and happy? That's because he eats everything *he* likes all day. He won't give me what I want, but you know how difficult humans can be. All I ask for is a little Beluga caviar on toast (I don't eat the toast but it looks pretty). Maybe some nice pâté de foie gras, lightly roasted pheasant (pink on the inside), and salmon garnished with rat gizzards. Of course, I may not eat *any* of it, but I'd at least like the right to turn it down. As you know, cats are the gourmets of the animal kingdom, but he insists on giving me kibble, surely the most plebian fare ever devised. I don't know how he expects me to eat that garbage day in and day out, even if it does have a pleasant stink, but I try to make him happy—he gets so excited when he puts it out for me that I hate to disappoint him. I guess I should have trained him better when he was younger.

Your nephew,
Puffy[2]

My objection to housework is that you spend hours getting everything sparkling clean, then have to do the whole thing over a year later.

WHEN JEHOVAH'S WITNESSES COME TO YOUR DOOR

- Tell them you're Jewish.
- Greet them naked holding a tube of K-Y jelly.
- Invite them into your coven.

A friend is upset because aliens never abduct her. "What's my DNA—chopped liver? What does Whitley Strieber have that I don't have?" I told her it's probably just not the right time yet.

Reptilians are people, too.

A channeled book said that the Pleiades are a more pleasant place to incarnate, with only 3% negativity

---

[2] Not his real name.

compared to our 47%. Whoa! Big difference.

It didn't say, however, whether they have high-speed Internet. If not, that's a deal-breaker. I don't care how much love and light they have—I'm not going to any more planets without it.

Some regard Earth as the insane asylum of the universe. A few of us rattle the bars, though.

You've probably heard the term "body, mind, and spirit."
That means your body is a temple,
and you shouldn't get drunk and throw up in it.
Once you're enlightened, though, what you drink, eat,
etc., won't matter, because you will transmute everything
to pure light. Amun-Ra, an Ascended Master
and former Egyptian god I used to know,[1]
eats only Dunkin' Donuts, and he possesses
all the secrets of the Universe.

However, until you reach that point
(probably at the end of this book),
it's not a bad idea to pay some attention to your health.
Here are some random thoughts on the subject.
It would be less disjointed if I hadn't run out of my pills.

---

[1] We went to Atlantis Junior High School together, and his locker was next to mine. I was a football star, and he was a total geek. Just goes to show you.

Chapter 6

HEALTH & DIET

My doctor told me that I have the body of a thirty-year-old. An out-of-shape, burnt-out thirty-year-old with bad genes, but still.

I'm one of those fortunate people who can eat anything I want—I just get really fat. That's why I started on the Fatkins Plan: high protein, fat, and carbs. It's very strict—you can't have any vegetables. It's shocking how many calories you save when you cut them out. (Did you ever read the label on a twenty-five pound bag of carrots?) However, they have some high-fat ice cream and cookies that taste just like them—I especially like the Brussels sprouts cookies—so you don't feel like you're missing out.

I do understand the anguish of eating disorders, though. Sometimes, I cannot force myself to eat more than ten or fifteen times a day.

I read that taking lecithin daily reduces chocolate cravings. Fortunately, my chocolate is already made with lecithin. When I learned about its benefits, I tripled my chocolate intake, and my cravings disappeared.

I've gotten down everything about dieting except the

part about eating less. It requires biting the bullet, and not much else.

However, I was glad to learn that I'm not overweight; I'm underheight. I simply need to be 6'9".

I'm a lacto-ovo-carno-vegetarian.

I love public radio's *The Splendid Table*, hosted by Lynne Rossetto Kasper, who answers questions from home cooks. Here's a recent one:

> Lynne, this is Patsy Sue from Dallas. I'm a member of a satanic cult, the Daughters of Cheney. Every year on the first full moon after the vernal equinox, we sacrifice a live baby and eat its brains. As you know, this is coming up soon. My problem is that those baby brains are so runny! I'm sure you've had this problem many times. I was wondering if you could recommend something.
>
> Also, what herbs would you use? I've always favored mugwort, but I'd like to surprise the girls this year and try something different. I was considering fresh basil pesto. Some of them like cilantro pesto, but I think that's just plain wrong. What is your opinion? Thank y'all.

When I fill out a form that asks for my family doctor, I write "Dr. Seuss."

I've been seeing commercials for several amazing drugs. They all show good-looking middle-aged people who are now carefree, walking hand-in-hand on the beach or in a meadow. ("Side effects may include vomiting, turning orange, or death.") One drug, though, has stood out. It's mentioned a lot, and seems to be pretty good for just about everything. For example, it enhances sexual performance when taken an hour before being with someone extremely hot. So I asked my doctor for a subscription. He gave me a magazine instead, which was full of drug ads; I'm not sure what he was trying to tell me. I wish they sold it outside the box.

Anyway, I'd recommend trying to get some of that Placebo stuff. I don't know what's in it, but it sure is helping people.

There's a Filipino psychic surgeon in Beverly Hills who does liposuction. He calls it "PsychoSuction." He also does nose jobs.

Once, while lying on an operating table (having a mole removed), I had a profound NLE (near-life experience). I went down a tunnel, saw a big dark blob, and felt pulled toward it until I heard a voice calling me back. Close call—I almost went into that body!

I joined a health club that promised I'd take off four

inches in three weeks. After a month, I'd gotten no results, but I still liked being a member and decided to start going.

I *did* get results from a new diet pill, BulimiSlim. You take one after every meal, and it makes you throw up. I lost two and a half inches—I'm now 5'7".

I discovered that health clubs don't work for me, so I'm getting an out-of-body personal trainer. The way it works is, you leave your body, the trainer comes into it, exercises it, then you come back and go about your day. No waiting in line for machines.

My friend the health nut will only smoke organic cigarettes.

A few weeks ago, my back went out and I haven't seen it since.

INTELLIGENT DESIGN

The design of humans is pretty intelligent, but I'd suggest some upgrades in Human 2.0, such as tailpipes that exude only clean water—like hydrogen cars. Knees and teeth could also use some work.

Bodies! Ya can't live with 'em, can't live without 'em!

INSOMNIA CURE

I decided to have a psychic phone reading with Sheila to see if she could figure out the reason for my insomnia. I felt that she really "got" me.

Right off the bat, she said to me—never having met me or seen my photo—"You're extremely good-looking, aren't you?"

"Why, yes," I replied.

"And everyone finds you utterly irresistible."

"Omigod! How did you know that?"

"I pick up that you have trouble sleeping."

"Yes, I do."

"It's because there are too many people in your bed—it makes it lumpy. Try sleeping with a few less people at a time, and you'll sleep fine."

I swear, all this *over the telephone!* I'm going to try her advice—I never would have thought of that.

Sex is a tricky subject when it comes to enlightenment.
The most basic question, of course, is
"Should I or shouldn't I?"

Some enlightened masters find no need for sex
whatsoever except with very cute young disciples.
However, the rest of us still have needs,
and there's nothing wrong with that.

The following chapter offers some thoughts
to consider when deciding what's right for you.

Chapter 7

SEX[1]

Abstinence is overrated. There's plenty of time to stop having sex after you're married. Why rush into that?

Both relationships and celibacy can be painful. You're screwed whether you're screwed or not.

A woman I knew was not only a tree-hugger but was in a long-term relationship with a redwood. She wanted someone big and hard. However, they had issues that finally splintered them apart.

I love porn. It has improved so much from the old days, when sometimes the urn would fall off your nightstand and break into several pieces. Frankly, the resolution wasn't great, either.

However, it's important to avoid the exploitation of women. Therefore, pornographers should focus exclusively on the all-male kind—men don't mind being sexually exploited at all.

A recent study showed that 79% of those with heterosexual partners found them to be problematic.

---

[1] This chapter is for ~~immature~~ mature audiences only.

As a result, experts now recommend that those seeking successful long-term relationships avoid straight people.

Dear Shepherd,

I loved your advice to "never marry a straight man," but I ask you, what's a girl to do?

You need a sensitive bisexual man who still likes women more. You know he's bisexual enough if he picks up his underwear. If the underwear is panties, he's definitely bisexual enough. On the other hand, if he yells at sporting events on TV, he's not bisexual enough unless perhaps he's wearing panties while he does it. Use your own discretion here.[2]

Do not judge a transvestite until you've walked a mile in his Manolo Blahniks.

One man's meat is a transsexual's poison.

---

[2] Just joking—the majority of cross-dressers are straight, and many macho guys who wear leather and drive Harleys are gay (not to mention lipstick lesbians). This is true even in the animal kingdom. Go figure—God is kinky. Archangel Michael told me that Jehovah Himself likes to wear fishnets and heels in the privacy of his own cloud; it gives him a welcome break from ruling the Universe.

A CONFESSION

You're no doubt aware from listening to crusaders for truth such as Rush Limbaugh that we homosexuals have been bent on converting all heterosexuals to our lifestyle (with the assistance of His Evilness, the Devil). I feel the need to come clean about my part in this:

I was an acquaintance of Dick Cheney's lovely daughter Mary, who was then a happily married housewife. However, I enticed her with one of our secret weapons, Portia de Rossi, and misused my psychic gifts to hypnotize her, so that now, she can no longer look at a naked man without throwing up. Mwahaha!

As time went by, though, I began to feel pangs of conscience, and worried what would happen if every woman were lesbian. Would millions of auto mechanics go out of business? Would Home Depots spread across the land like a blotchy orange rash? If so, how could I live with myself? And what if every man started having brunch and being fabulous? Would Bed Bath & Beyonds be stampeded and destroyed? Would there be a dire shortage of skin care products?

Therefore, I conferred with my homosexual brothers and sisters, and we decided that when we are done taking over the world, we are going to make conversion optional. We have come to realize that each person has something special to offer, even fashion-challenged males and females lacking in mechanical aptitude. There is a place for everyone under the rainbow flag.

HOT GAY MORMON SEX

I had a friend who had come out, left the Mormon church, and decided to make up for lost time by sleeping with at least one different man a night. He told me that by 2 a.m., there was always someone to go home with at the Boom Boom Room. I admired his goal-setting skills and tenacity. And he still had a wholesome, boy-next-door quality, despite being a total slut—that shows he was brought up right.

Conservatives worry that gay marriage will lead to people marrying their dogs. What's wrong with that? In my book, if your dog is able to stand and say, "I do," he's earned the right to marry.

How wonderful that flab is the new muscle. Finally, the soft, cuddly body type is the beau ideal, and the perfect pear-shaped body is worshipped. It wasn't long ago, believe it or not, when people thought that hard, lumpy muscles and boring, flat stomachs were attractive! Fortunately, that fad passed, along with the unappetizing sweating and grunting they require. Emergency room visits due to partners with "cut" physiques have dropped by over 50%. We've returned to a kinder, gentler sensibility that reveres carb-loving epicures such as Santa Claus, the Buddha, and Jabba the Hutt. Thank goodness we no longer idolize violent body-builders who eat more bloody flesh than cavemen, threaten to be back, and run for governor.

Dirty old men and women have needs, too.

Mae West after enlightenment: "Is that a crystal in your pocket, or are you just glad to see me?"

Maya is Sanskrit for "illusion." Physical attractiveness is part of the maya of the physical plane—one of my favorite parts.

We humans make such a ruckus
Trying to get someone to f*ckus.

If you're not having any luck finding your soul mate and it's been more than five years, you can become a virgin again through the Virginity Renewal program of the Department of Abstinence Education (established by the Bush administration). The physical exam alone is worth the $49 application fee.

HELPFUL HINT FROM MARTHA

Do you want your buttocks to smell like a rose garden? Eat potpourri before bed. Your fragrance will bring pleasure to your partner all night long. Remember: it's not gas—it's aromatherapy.

Getting older is the single biggest thing
you can do to reach enlightenment.
If that doesn't work,
at least you're not dead yet.

Chapter 8

AGING

When you get to be as old as I am, you start to ponder the big questions, such as "How did I get to be so #*¢king old!?"

A friend is remembering me in her living will. When she goes, I get her gall bladder.

I made a living will, too. The only heroic last-minute procedures I'll allow are liposuction and a face lift.

I'm a late bloomer; I get better the more decrepit I become. By the time I'm disgusting, I'll be fabulous!

Aging is strange. It happens to everyone (who doesn't, of course, die first) but it still puzzles us. I'm, what? seventy or ninety now (who can remember?) but inside, I feel thirty. I understand now why my grandma used to tell me she felt young inside. "But Grandma," I'd say, "you act like you're a hundred." She never wanted to do anything. She sat on the couch all day watching TV until she bored a hole in it (the couch, not the TV). At least I get off my couch sometimes and go sit on a recliner. In fact, since variety and change keep you young, I have four recliners, and move from one to another. That's how I stay sharp.

Enlightened beings are naturally philosophical.
Once people know you're enlightened,
they'll expect you to say wise things.
Here are a few to choose from:

Chapter 9

WORDS TO LIVE BY

Never give a blow job to a rattlesnake.

If you're going to lose your Self, be sure to leave a forwarding address.

A big fish in a small pond is still a fish.

Better laid than never.

You should *never* use the word "should."

He who dances with a porcupine gets stuck.

Savor each day—you only live a few hundred times.

Do not do today what you can put off until another lifetime.

You didn't believe in reincarnation in your last lifetime, either.

No man is an island. Some men, however, are Nebraska.

PART II

THE PHYSICAL PLANE

It has long been predicted
that California will fall into the ocean.
Some people thought I was crazy to leave a safe place
like New York City and move to Laguna.
However, I knew it was right to be here,
and to reach enlightenment,
you have to trust your intuition.
So far, I'm pleased with my choice.
I'm not dead yet, and I think that speaks for itself.

Chapter 10

EARTH CHANGES & CALIFORNIA

Synchronicities often reveal divine guidance operating in our lives. For instance, one day, a friend had a dream about an earthquake occurring where I live in Southern California; the next, an offer to buy earthquake insurance came in the mail. It just goes to show that when God closes a door, He opens a window, and then smashes it.

As you know, however, affirmations can help you create the reality you wish to live in, so I've been affirming, "I'm too young to die, I'm too young to die" and "Everybody but me is falling into the ocean."

Come to think of it, I joked about earthquakes in Atlantis, too, so maybe this isn't a good idea. Never mind.

Still, I'm not all that worried about earthquakes here. For one thing, just as Virginia has Pat Robertson to pray for it, we in Orange County have Robert Schuller of the Crystal Cathedral, conveniently located near Disneyland. It has world-famous Christmas and Easter pageants featuring a huge choir, orchestra, and livestock. You can imagine how powerful and inspiring that place is. Schuller, the author of bestsellers about love, was arrested for slugging a flight attendant in first class, but if he's a personal friend of Jesus, that's good enough for me. I'm sure it's no coincidence that he owns a condo where I used to live. I once invited him over for some channeling and a burnt offering (barbecue), but unfortunately, he was busy.

Another reason I'm not nervous about living here is that wise beings on higher planes have said that you can be safe in California as long as you religiously back up your hard drive and send the disks to Colorado, which I do.

ADVENTURES WITH FURNITURE

When I moved here, I needed some new furniture. I bought an inexpensive dresser and carefully tied it to the luggage rack of my car; it was exciting to finally get to use it. I tucked the excess rope under it and left for home. After stopping for a signal, two cars behind me drove over the long rope now trailing me. When the light changed and I continued forward, the dresser flew off. I'm very proud of how tightly I tied down the dresser, proven by the fact that the rack came off, too. Frankly, however, I'm appalled at the poor crash testing of dressers in this country.

I also bought a used Italian leather couch, but it was too big to get through the doorway. I guess that in Italy, they make the couches first, then build the houses around them. We hoisted it up a story over the railing of my terrace. At one point, we were hanging onto it for dear life. Fortunately, I'm a very macho guy, and the maintenance man was able to help out after I burst into tears.

That move was expensive and difficult, but I learned that the Universe always provides: in another one of those amazing synchronicities, I was approved for a new credit card *and* met a bankruptcy lawyer the same week.

Driving is a necessity here, and I'm a pretty good driver—I haven't hit anyone in ages, except one time last year, and that old lady had no business being in the crosswalk! This is California, for chrissakes. No one walks anywhere, except at the gym.

Some religious people believe that California's earthquakes, fires, and mudslides are God's punishment for promiscuity, gays, and the porn industry. I channeled about this issue and learned, to my surprise, that that is indeed the case. The earthquakes, fires, and mudslides that occurred in California before humans lived here were because the plants and animals were also too promiscuous. God especially doesn't like it when birds and bees have sex outside marriage—He feels it sets a bad example.

Now, let's get down
to the nitty-gritty
of everyday enlightenment.

Chapter 11

A MOVING STORY

Moving is said to be one of the five most stressful things in life, along with the death of a loved one, bankruptcy, divorce, and Republicans.[1]

For one thing, we accumulate so much stuff. During my most recent move, I decided to carefully sort through everything, and it took weeks. Toward the end, the Chinese owner of the liquor store where I got boxes looked at me incredulously and asked, "You *still* moving?"

Incidentally, when a friend moved, he labeled a box of wedding silver "SILVER," and it never arrived—the movers stole it. So I labeled all my boxes "CR*P" and "MORE CR*P."

In dealing with stress, I'm a big believer in practicing mindfulness as an alternative to Stoli. I do admit, though, that one evening, I downed two quarts of Very Cherry Chip Soy Cream in a relatively short period of time, but that was because there wasn't anything else

---

[1] If you're reading this book, then by definition, you are on your way to enlightenment. If you happen to be a Republican, you are the non-stressful kind who believes in equal rights for gays and women, and helping the poor, although in fiscally responsible ways. Therefore, this joke does not apply to you.

On the other hand, if you're not reading this book, doing so would be a sound investment, certain to make you even richer than you already are.

to eat. With the bowls still packed, I had to eat it directly from the carton; it was impossible not to finish it since I was in an easy chair and couldn't get up. Add the fact that children are starving in Africa, and you can clearly see it wasn't my fault.

This time, the movers were able to get the couch in through the front picture window (brilliant!)—it was open, by the way—with nary a scratch. If not quite poetry, it was prose in motion.

Unfortunately, things were not so smooth for the marble-top coffee table, perhaps because it isn't Italian. However, there's always a silver lining: it was very heavy; in five pieces, it was easier to transport.

Previously, when I disassembled my AV and computer set-ups, I was daunted by the endless cords and adapters tangled in a dusty Dr. Seuss-like maze. I figured it would take divine or cable company intervention to get it all working again at my new place.

Then I realized—I don't mean to boast—that being a very old soul, I've had a *lot* of past lives in consumer electronics. In fact, in one lifetime, I was a cable installer. Back in those days, we used jute instead of coaxial, but I don't think things have otherwise changed that much. I knew that if I could go into a deep enough trance, I could access my inner knowledge.

I'm pleased to report that I got the AV set-up working fine with only the aid of some medicinal substances, and was able to streamline it, reducing the number of cords to under a hundred fifty.

I also easily got my Internet access up and running, with only four customer-service-erased emails, three outages, two password changes, and a cable chewed in half by some bird in a tree.

Of course, getting everything else put together had a few hitches, too. For example, a little thingy fell out of the futon frame, and it could not be reassembled without it. When hunting for parts in hardware stores, one is reminded of an important enlightenment lesson: little things mean a lot. If you can't find the right screw, you're screwed. International standards reducing the number of types to the essentials would increase efficiency a good deal. The screw industry could use the motto, "Less screwing around, more screwing."

My previous place was on the ocean, and that's hard to beat. However, there are some pluses here, too. For example, in my old place, the bedrooms faced Coast Highway and had frosted windows. Here, from the bedrooms, there's a pretty view of a verdant hillside, lush trees, a parking lot, and a dumpster.

On the path to enlightenment,
we can receive profound messages anywhere,
from the glance of a stranger on a bus,
a song playing on the radio at just the right time,
or an overflowing porcelain lavatory fixture.

Chapter 12

MY TOILET RUNNETH OVER

When I moved, I was thankful for having a toilet that worked right. The old one was always getting clogged.

Then, after a month, the toilet in my new place started getting clogged, too. I wondered what was going on. Why had I been creating overflowing toilets wherever I went?

I looked it up in Louise Hay under "Toilet, Stopped-up," and she said that it demonstrated my unwillingness to let go of old issues. Gosh, I thought I was willing, but maybe I wasn't. After all, toilets don't lie. I called a plumber—I needed to get to the bottom of this.

He snaked it and found a bundle of floss. Uh-oh. Yes, I'd thrown some in without giving it a second thought. It was Glide floss, which was clearly a misnomer. Of course, I demanded my money back.

A domestic god/dess's work is never done.
However, every experience is grist
for the enlightenment mill.

Chapter 13

A LESSON IN IMPATIENCE

After I got settled, I decided to paint the bathrooms, since the color looked like urine. Perhaps that was poetically appropriate, but I'm an autumn, and of course, urine is a spring color. I figured it would take about a day. Instead, it took six, not including cleanup. I wonder if God thought it would take Him a day to create the world. "Some oceans, some mountains, a sentient monkey without hair. What could be so hard?" Of course, God didn't speak English then; he would have said it in Yiddish. And He's still working on cleanup, so maybe I shouldn't complain.

Part of the problem was that one bathroom has a cathedral ceiling, and in my innocence, I decided to use three different colors: sage, camel, and white. These needed to meet in straight lines twelve feet off the ground. My ladder is six feet, but I had poles and special attachments that promised to perfectly paint those hard-to-reach corners.

If you define "straight" as a one out of six on the Kinsey scale of sexual orientation, my lines, after much effort, came down from a four to maybe a two and a half. Where's Focus on the Family when you need it? They claim to be able to turn a six into a one.

After I was done, I didn't like the "Desert Camel" that much—the chip book was better than the wall movie. Still, it was satisfying to say "Camel enamel" and ponder why Home Depot named it "*Desert* Camel."

Maybe they wanted to differentiate it from Rain Forest Camel (four humps) and Alpine Meadow Camel (three). Or perhaps they wanted to be clear that it wasn't Nicotine Camel.

As the pages of the calendar rapidly flipped over, I started to fear that I'd be painting these two bathrooms for the rest of my life. Furthermore, I might have to come back for another lifetime just to finish them. I'd never again walk on the beach or eat out. My only link to the outside world would be the telephone and restaurants that deliver. I wouldn't be able to read a book or watch a movie; I'd be doomed to a purgatory of an endless loop of NPR pledge drives. All my hopes and dreams would go down the drain with the milky green and yellow paintbrush water. I was starting to lose it—can you become delirious from latex vapors?

Then suddenly, an angel appeared unto me. She said, "Beloved One, patience is one of life's most important lessons. You *will* finish painting the bathrooms someday. You'll look back and have a good laugh about how the painter's tape guaranteed not to pull off the paint pulled off the paint, how you burned your arm on the bare bulb, how you stayed up until 4 a.m., ..."

This wasn't helping, but I didn't want to be impolite—it's not every day an angel comes unto you.

She continued, "Take a deep breath, and visualize the fumes filling every cell of your body. Now affirm: 'I live in the now. I am at peace. I am patience personified.'"

"I live in the now. I am at peace. I am patience personified. I am patience personified." I could sense something shifting within me. Finally, it broke free.

"The h*ck with that!" Standing in the bathtub, I shook my roller toward Heaven. (Actually, it was toward the cathedral ceiling. Close enough—cathedrals are supposed to bring you nearer to God, right?) I was wearing nothing but paint-splattered underwear and a plastic shower cap, in addition to yellow rubber gloves and a green mask, which, of course, matched the new color scheme. Surely I was a fearsome sight before the Lord. (Earlier, a friend of my roommate screamed when he saw me.)

I cried out with a loud voice, in the Biblical manner, saying, "Why is everything so d*rn slow on the physical plane? On the astral plane, when I want different colored walls, all I have to do is think them. And why, when you go over and over a corner spot on textured surfaces, does it stay white, but the wall you're avoiding gets a perfect one-coat finish? Whose idea was textured walls anyway? Is this as far as all these eons of evolution have brought us? #*¢k this! I'm going to a different planet."

That told God! I felt a lot better.

So if you're struggling with impatience, just give in to it and go totally berserk. You'll be glad you did.

I gotta go. The washer/dryer repairman is coming for the fifth time. Plus, I think I'll paint the kitchen. It needs a little color.

We all suffer setbacks, but when life hands you lemons, you can make the lemon meringue pie of enlightenment. Here's an example of how I did it.

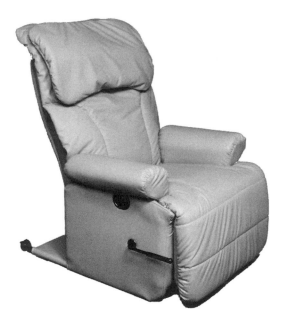

Chapter 14

GAINING PERSPECTIVE

I had finally recovered from painting the bathrooms when tragedy struck—my beloved Panasonic Massage Lounger died. This was not unexpected, though; the remote had been acting erratically. Still, nothing can prepare you for the finality of the end.

I went through the five stages of grief:

DENIAL:
No, my chair can't be dead.

ANGER:
Panasonic, you XIDLELSLL21!!!@@@@xyyysyy!

BARGAINING:
Okay, I'll get it fixed. It will cost how much?

DEPRESSION:
Oh, h*ck.

ACCEPTANCE:
Okay, I'll replace it.

You know how when you hear about other people who have problems far worse than your own, yours come into perspective? If there's a silver lining in all this, it's that other people might learn about what I've been through and say to themselves, "I may have lost a limb or be living on the street in a cardboard box, but *at least my Panasonic Massage Lounger didn't die.*" If that happens, it will have all been worth it.

Fortunately, God was watching over me. Someone on Craigslist was selling one just like mine, but newer, for $275. The owner didn't get my first email, and she had gotten several calls, but no one showed up before I did—God was saving it for me and tied up everyone else in bad traffic.

AN UPDATE: I bought my new Panasonic Massage Lounger during a Mercury Retrograde. An astrologer friend had warned me never to do anything during a Mercury Retrograde. She doesn't even go to the bathroom during one—she holds it. Sure enough, two Mercury Retrogrades later, my new chair also died. I've learned my lesson: from now on, I'm staying under my bed until Mercury goes direct.

This is an age of miraculous advancements.
Today's technology has vastly simplified life,
giving you more time to devote to enlightenment,
even providing tools for attaining it.

On the other hand,
progress sometimes comes with a glitch or two.

Chapter 15

POPULAR MECHANICS

Machines breaking down help teach you forbearance. Clearly, this is one of God's favorite lessons for me. It wasn't just my Panasonic Massage Loungers, but for a while, almost every mechanical device I came near.

For instance, I had an expensive stereo receiver that developed a hum. I spent $100 to have it repaired, but it still hummed. I then spent hours checking connections, speakers, other components, etc. I finally got rid of the hum—I threw the receiver into the ocean.

Challenges like this have given me huge growth opportunities, and don't think I'm not grateful.

However, I'm happy to report that I'm no longer a helpless victim of things breaking down all around me; now, I'm destroying them myself.

For example, I killed my air conditioner when I hosed it down from outside. I had a momentary thought that I should turn it off first, but then decided, "Nah, it's built to withstand rain." I do feel good about the fact that when I put it in the dumpster, it was extremely clean.

I also left my car's dome light on and ran down the battery (for the third or fourth time). I called AA, and they sent out an anonymous man, "Mike," to jump it. He encouraged me to acknowledge that I was powerless in the face of battery failure and needed to submit it to a higher power. I broke down crying, and told him about the air conditioner and receiver.

I can't say for sure that I'll never leave on the dome light again; it's one day at a time.

I love television, but sometimes there's nothing to watch, and I have to surf the web or watch movies instead. Recently, it has gotten so bad that I've almost been forced to read a book. I hope it doesn't come to that.

My favorite television drama is CSI: SUV. It investigates brutal, inexplicable crimes that occur in sports utility vehicles. The next episode guest stars Tommy Smothers and Sally Struthers as drive-through clerks taking orders for more than just burgers.

It's important to let go of attachments. For that reason, I rarely send them with emails.

When you log onto AOL, you hear a perky voice saying, "Welcome! You've Got Mail!" Wouldn't it be nice if, instead, they gave you a different, pertinent message each time? Here are a few suggestions:

- Welcome! You've got spam!
- Welcome! You've got syphilis!
- Welcome! You've got tomato sauce on your shirt!

• Welcome! You've got to start working out, girl.

Crumbs from cookies deposited by web sites can slow down your computer. It helps to occasionally take the case off and hose it down. Then, set your browser to accept only chocolate chip cookies; at least the mess will be worth it.

If you're having trouble with your Windows computer, here's an easy two-step procedure that will solve your problems:

1. Drag it to the Recycle Bin.
2. Buy a Mac.

Frankly, I don't completely understand Facebook. For one thing, I was raised never to write on my wall. Also, my nephew asked me to send him a chicken for Farmville, so I went to a farm and got him one. I packed her carefully, but the post office wouldn't take her—they said she was too old. Isn't that ageism? Even worse, they looked at me like I was a terrorist trying to mail a chicken of mass destruction.

When the chicken started tweeting, I thought maybe she was trying to tell me I should be using Twitter instead, which I also don't entirely understand.

I may be hopelessly out-of-touch, but what's wrong with good old-fashioned email? It was good enough for my grandpappy. I see kids texting all day. Their thumbs are no longer opposable. They're ruining thousands of years of evolution! Isn't it faster just to call? I don't get it.

Europe is on the metric system, which tends to confuse Americans. For instance, in the U.S., we have a chain of convenience stores called "7-Eleven"; in Europe, they're called "0.636363."

European days are divided into a hundred metric hours ("centipedes"); instead of a watch, people there wear a pedometer. I learned that in fifth grade (.2 grade metric).

Here are some outgoing voicemail messages I've used over the years:

• Hi! You've reached 428-3792. I'm out of my body right now and can't get to the phone, but if you'll leave a message, I'll get back to you when I return.

• Please leave a brief message after the tone, including your name, home number, work number, cell number, fax number, social security number, web site address, email address, Facebook address, Twitter address, MySpace address, IP address, snail mail address, and favorite fruit. Thanks.

• This is Jehovah. I'm out of my office until Tuesday but I'll be checking messages daily, so please leave your prayer after the chord.

Ouija boards are iPhones to the Other Side, but you have to be careful with them. If you use one left-handed, you could lose the signal; sometimes a case helps. If you're getting weird information, you may need a new battery. If that doesn't work, exchange it for a new one.

PART III

SPIRITUAL ARTS
&
SCIENCES

People in Asia are simply more enlightened
than those of us in the West.
For instance, in China almost every restaurant
serves feng shui (which is delicious with rice).

Of course, India is the capital of enlightenment.
There you can find gurus
who bilocate *without* FaceTime,
and live hundreds of years in the same village
with only minimal plastic surgery.

Chapter 16

BREATHARIANS & SUN GAZERS

A friend of mine knows a breatharian, someone who doesn't eat but instead derives his nourishment through long sessions of deep breathing. There are several accounts of breatharians in India. My friend's friend has a glass of juice every week or so, but many there are said to have had no food at all for years other than an occasional Big Mac.

Less known are sun gazers, who get their nourishment by staring at it, without damaging their eyes.

I wonder ... When it's overcast for several days, do sun gazers starve? Can they feed off solar panels? Does their food channel broadcast the sunrise 24/7?

Do some people live off both sun and breath? Let's say it's a special occasion and a group of breatharians and sun gazers go out for brunch. Would having both be like a buffet? If they breathe while sunning, do they get indigestion?

If breatharians need to lose weight, do they breathe less? How many calories does air have? Is it less fattening than sunshine? What do they have for dessert? If they go on a fast, do they eat food?

Do self-destructive breatharians breathe bus fumes? Do self-sacrificing breatharians say, "I don't need any air today—you go ahead and finish it"?

Are there other non-food items one can live on, like dirt?

Food for thought.

Astrology is perhaps the most indispensible tool
for enlightened people.
For example, it was astrolovematch.com
that told me Brad Pitt is my soul mate—
it was astoundingly accurate.

Chapter 17

ASTROLOGY

This is a particularly difficult time astrologically—the Moon is in the Dog House.

It's well known that when Mercury goes backward in the sky, communication can be fouled up.

Romeo and Juliet is a classic tale of what happens when you try to make plans during a Mercury Retrograde. That was what Shakespeare meant when he called them "star-crossed lovers." Had Mercury been direct, Romeo would have gotten the message that Juliet wasn't dead, just drugged. They would have lived long enough for Juliet to learn that Romeo was a slob who left his tights on the bathroom floor, and for Romeo to taste Juliet's rubbery lasagna. They might have killed themselves on purpose, but they never got the chance.

The obvious lesson is that you ignore astrology at your own peril.

Someone told me that there was a new moon last night, but I couldn't see it.

Good feng shui can make
your environment more peaceful
so you aren't distracted from becoming enlightened.
It's based on the five *elements*
of water, fire, rock, paper, and scissors.

Chapter 18

FENG SHUI

had my place feng shuied by an expert. There were only a couple significant problems, which can be fixed fairly easily. Basically, the water is where the fire should be, and the fire is where the water should be. Therefore, I'm having the toilet installed where the stove is, and vice versa. I'm sure my landlord won't mind, since it will so improve the flow of chi.

Crop circles are one of many signs from above that can help direct you toward enlightenment. However, they are controversial.

Chapter 19

CROP CIRCLES: The Truth Revealed!

LONDON—A British spiritualist, Henrietta Wigsby-Covington-Mayfair (known as the English Channel), announced on the telly this morning that, according to her spirit guide Horse Feather, most crop circles are hoaxes perpetrated by Sasquatch. "We need to catch that hairy brute, and soon," she said, "before all our farmers join cults and stop doing their chores. Then where would we be?

"I'm sympathetic that Mr. Sasquatch can't go back to Maldek, seeing how it's smashed up and all, but he should get his big sweaty feet out of our crops and find a different creative outlet, maybe needlepoint or woodworking. Farms are no place for self-expression. It's not proper."

When Cedric Humpington, host of "Good Morning Worcestershire-Upon-Rutland-on-Thames," asked her about the rumor that crop circles are created by extraterrestrials, she replied, "Many of us are extra-terrestrials, lovey. I'm Pleiadian myself. However, you've a good point. Some of those spaceships have been doodling in our fields, too. Those little gray people get so bored cooped up in their smelly ships; it's a bit of amusement for them, like teens spraying graffiti on schoolyard walls saying 'Vark was here.' The blue aliens never make circles—they haven't an artistic bone in their bodies; they're worse than Microsoft and the British Accounting Association put together. And the green ones are deathly afraid of wheat. Most of it is Sasquatch, although he'd like you to think otherwise. He's been stealing vegetables from my garden, too, bending my chard and scaring my poor kitty Emma half to death. It's got to stop, I tell you."

PART IV

THE AMERICAS

Asia has certainly been the big winner
in the Enlightenment Olympics,
but several cultures in North and South America
have fared impressively as well.

You may not be aware, for example,
that there are twenty-story pyramids in Mexico
that the Mayans imported from Egypt
over a thousand years ago.
Some of them even have satellite TV and walk-in closets.

The Mayans were also trailblazers
in the calendar business.

Chapter 20

THE MAYAN CALENDAR

Someone asked me to channel about why the Mayan calendar ended in 2012. Doreen explained that it was because they ran out of paper. The kind they favored, with a row of little holes across the top, was hard to find—they hadn't yet discovered OfficeMax.

Of course, in our culture, we only print our calendars a year in advance. The reason they decided to do their entire future calendar at once is that the printer offered them a 15% discount.

Another factor was that the official calendar featured the Sacrificial Virgin of the Month. Since there were not enough of them to have a unique one every month for the foreseeable future, they dressed them up in a variety of costumes. With changes in make-up and lighting, you couldn't tell the difference. However, when the shamans went into trance to foretell what Sacrificial Virgins would be wearing each year, they were stumped when they got to Project Runway. It was like the Native Americans who couldn't see Columbus's ships because they had no frame of reference. Rather than publishing a calendar that might have out-of-date fashions, and considering the paper situation, they decided to cap it at 2012.

Another great civilization was the Incas.
Their magnificent city Machu Picchu
is a must-see for all seekers.
If you weren't enlightened before you got there,
you're sure to be once you are.

Here's a bit of interesting trivia about it:

Chapter 21

MACHU PICCHU

Many people are curious how Machu Picchu got its name. According to Doreen, Machu Picchu is Peruvian for "Macho Peaches." Several hundred years ago, the area was filled with peach orchards.

They grew a particular variety, now extinct, that was big and low hanging, and grew in pairs. Every year, the people had a peach festival that lasted three days. The women put up large amounts of peach preserves for the coming winter in Balls canning urns, and it is said that their peach cobbler has not been equaled since. This is understandable, considering that they made it on one of earth's premier power spots using strictly organic ingredients.

The highlight of the festival was an orgy during which they smeared peaches all over each other and ate them off. After about a century, this practice was discontinued when they realized why so many people were getting rashes.

Of course, no enlightened person would be caught dead
without at least one Native American spirit guide.
Native peoples lived in perfect harmony
with all the beings of the earth and sky
when they weren't killing each other.

I was trained in their ways from an early age.

Chapter 22

MY NATIVE AMERICAN ROOTS

When I was five, my dad took me to Indian Guides meetings in the lodge of one of my schoolmates. My Indian name was "Little Chief Catsup Head" because of my red hair. (The proper Native American spelling was "Ketchup," but the Indian Guides weren't sticklers about such things.) In addition to my keen interest at that age in shamanism, what I most liked was that they served Coke and buffalo chip cookies afterward. The delicious cookies, from an authentic recipe, were made from a combination of corn and maize.

PART V

GETTING DOWN
TO BUSINESS

Everything new is old again.
As you become enlightened,
you enter a brave new world
uniting the mysticism of our ancestors
with the pragmatism of business.
Today, lightworkers are bringing light to work,
and trade organizations such as Prophets for Profit
demonstrate how to get rich *and* save humanity.

I hope my new business will show you
that with a little pluck and vision,
the world can be your soyster.

Chapter 23

BED DEATH & **BEYOND**

I'm starting a chain of stores called "Bed Death & Beyond." They will feature an array of caskets, mattresses, movies and books, crystal balls, and skeletons. I'm creating a Do-It-Yourself Near-Death-Experience Kit, with a workbook, DVD, and CosmoGlasses™ (batteries and knife not included). We're also in discussions with the Kevorkian and Hemlock Society people about carrying their products. Spiritual Genius Bars will offer consultations with on-staff mediums, channels, dowsers, and oracles. BD&B will truly offer "One-stop shopping for all your death needs."

There will be séance rooms with daily events. I'm inviting prominent rappers such as 50 Cent and Snoop Dogg to help launch them: "This is not your grandmother's séance."

Reincarnational counselors will be available to help you plan your next lifetime, and reservations will be accepted for bodies through 2075 with a 30% deposit: "Act now before all the good ones are taken!"

Our exclusive Out-of-Body Travel Agency will offer guided tours of the astral plane, with stops in Heaven, Hell, Purgatory, Paradise, Existential Nothingness, and other fun destinations: "Go to Hell—and get a companion ticket absolutely free!"

Purchases of over $1000 are eligible for the innova-tive Karmic Repayment Plan, in which you can buy now and pay in your next lifetime. Coffins can be purchased on layaway. Also, be sure to visit our Cryogenics Center and Undead Pavilion: "Eternity is forever."

Text me if you'd like to invest in this exciting venture. You'll make a killing! Death is hot, with television shows like *Medium, Ghost Whisperer,* and *Six Feet Under.* Remember: "The Other Side isn't just for dead people anymore."

The business world seems full of stuffed shirts,
but you might be surprised what you find there.

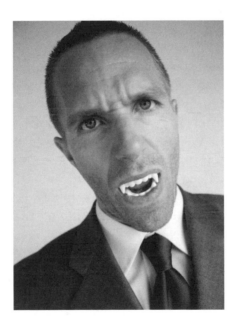

Chapter 24

IN OTHER BUSINESS NEWS ...

I t was revealed today that Bill Gates is, in fact, richer than God. According to financial statements released this morning, Gates's personal net worth is $54 billion, for the first time edging out God. God blamed the drop in His portfolio on the continuing worldwide banking crisis, the Catholic church's pedophilia scandal, and the end of *The Oprah Winfrey Show*.

A Microsoft spokesperson also confirmed a rumor that had been flying around the blogosphere for months: Gates is competitive with God in another respect, eternal life—Gates is a vampire. A representative of WAVES, the Werewolf and Vampire Education Society, applauded the announcement. "For centuries, undead persons have been stigmatized. We're thrilled that such an exemplary citizen as Mr. Gates has come out. He reminds us all that those who happen to sleep during the day and drink blood deserve full equal rights."

Karl "Jedi" Cohen, popular CoolStuff blogger at geek.com, said, "Sweet! Having $54 billion and never dying—what could be better? Forever gives you a lot of time for video games. I already stay up all night. I wonder if I could get Bill to bite me and give me some money."

Although Gates has formally stepped down as CEO of Microsoft, investors enthusiastically greeted the news that he would be around to guide its course in perpetuity. Its stock was up by over seven points in heavy trading.

One of Gates's former associates, who spoke on condition of anonymity, said, "I don't care about people's personal lifestyles as long as they deliver results. I always thought Bill looked kind of pale, and sometimes he'd show up at meetings with drops of blood on his chin—I figured he'd cut himself shaving.

"Now that I think about it, I'd bet many CEOs are vamps, not that there's anything wrong with that. They're human, too. Actually, they aren't, but you need sharp teeth to get ahead in this global economy. Anyway, Bill's announcement in no way changes my opinion of him, and I'm sure I'm joined by my colleagues in wishing him the best of luck."

You don't create your own reality in a vacuum;
you rely on help from your spirit guides,
angels, personal assistants, and other staff.

This is a piece I wrote in my business column
for *EarthToday* about the back office.

Chapter 25

OUTSOURCING & UFOS

You've probably noticed that in recent decades, customer service in the Universe has sharply deteriorated. For instance, I know someone who asked the Universe for a million dollars over thirty years ago, and she's still waiting! That never would have happened a few generations ago. Of course, a few generations ago, she probably would have been dead by now, but still.

At the same time, there has been a large increase in UFO sightings all over the world. It's not a coincidence. Here's the story:

In addition to the population explosion in general, there are rapidly expanding numbers of people trying to create a more abundant reality with the help of the Universe. It started small, with winning friends and influencing people. Then it moved into positive thinking. When Oprah went into syndication, there was no turning back, and then came *The Secret*. Once, that was an ice-blue deodorant whose only goal was to keep people cool, calm, and collected, but now it promises the sky.

It's not hard to understand the appeal of this trend. The generic default human reality is pretty crummy—quality control has been atrocious, and human investment in R&D has been minimal. The relentless focus on the bottom line has resulted in appalling short-sightedness that has imperiled this planet's very existence. So it's natural that people want to upgrade to a premium reality if they can, and the consciously create-your-own option is becoming increasingly compelling: the advent of prenups has put a damper on marrying for money, plus there's a growing awareness that money can't buy happiness unless it's accompanied by tight abs.

However, the predictable result of so many do-it-yourselfers is that the Universe's tech support and customer service centers are severely overworked and spread thin. Stress levels for angels and spirit guides have skyrocketed—expectations are so high that spirit guides now need their own spirit guides to cope.

For example, miracles used to be for special occasions, like new scriptures and photo-ops. Now, however, people want every cold eliminated in seconds. Sure, many used to ask for peace on earth once a year, but they didn't really mean it. Throughout much of history, most people were happy with their guides if no one found out about their illegitimate children or they didn't die of the Plague. Today, people expect a soul mate who is physically fit and will cater to their every need without being asked. In addition, they demand a successful career of their own choice and a flat screen television double their waist size. No wonder so many celestial helpers are burning out, and few newborn souls are going into the business, either. Until the recent recession, a number of guides took on human bodies themselves—after helping some of their former clients get rich, they decided to try their own luck at it. Of course, it's not as easy as it looks.

What does this have to do with UFOs? God, the charismatic CEO of the Universe, was forced by market conditions to start outsourcing.

There are many people on much more technologically advanced planets who would be bored to tears if they still had emotions. Their reality shows consist of robots drilling for metals on smoking ruins of planets. God rightly figured that they would find Earth's residents more entertaining than that. Having a hands-on experience would be even more interesting. So God created a reality show, "Survivor: Earth."

The extraterrestrials signed on to help with customer support here, answering prayers, offering guidance, and that sort of thing. The deal is that whoever lasts the longest and can still pass a sanity test will win 500 million kilos of zinc, which is worth about $125 billion. As you can see, the stakes are high.

God lets them record it for the viewers back home (all those flying saucers are equipped with high-def 5-D cameras). The highlights collection on orange-ray is already the all-time bestseller in several galaxies, in both comedy and drama.

It's a win-win: the Universe gets much-needed staffing; extraterrestrials get entertainment and minerals.

However, the contestants are dropping like flies, and no one yet knows God's plan for when the game is over. There is speculation that at least some former guides will want their jobs back after some intensive therapy, especially considering current economic conditions. Let's hope so.

The ETs had already been studying us, so they quickly became fluent in our languages. The big problem for Earthlings with outsourcing has been the poor training. In the past, angels and guides had centuries of preparation and apprenticeship. Today, they are rushed into service after a few days, and often have to read from scripts. Every time a cell phone rings, an angel gets his wings, but it doesn't mean anything anymore—angels get wings now just for showing up to work sober.

An account in one of our blogs, the Wilson Report, illustrates the issues:

In my distress I cried out, "Help me, God! Why is this happening to me?"

After years of feeling alone in the Universe, I suddenly heard a still small voice. There's someone out there!

"I'm so sorry you're having trouble with the physical plane today. But don't worry—everything is for a reason."

"Thank you! Thank you very much," I replied. "That's a real comfort ... but what's the reason?"

He frantically clicked buttons trying to find in the database where it would tell him what to say. Then, "Please hold." Several minutes passed. "Thank you very much for holding. The reason is that you have lessons to learn."

"What lessons?"

"Please hold." The angelic music came on. Then I was cut off.

I called out again.

"You've reached the Universe. For quality purposes, your call may be recorded or monitored. For Earthling, press 1; for Martian, 2. Thank you. Please enter your forty-nine digit soul number." I shuffled through my papers and finally found it. "For customer service, press 1; for technical support, 2; for karmic bill repayments, 3; to complain about the weather, 4; to complain about significant others and family members, 5; for all other complaints, 6; and for winning lotto numbers, 7. For extension 8, please press 9. If this is an emergency, hang up and call the Angelic Special Weapons and Tactics Unit at 1-777-SWAT-911."

I pressed 2. I then listened to twenty-seven minutes of music interrupted by announcements about special growth opportunities.

"Thank you for calling Heaven. This is John. How may I be of service?"

I explained everything from the beginning.

"Please hold. ... Thank you for holding. I have the answer for you. You need to learn patience."

"Oh. Well, that's true. I guess you're right. I'll work on it. Thanks."

"Is there anything else I can help you with?"

"No, that's fine. Thank you very much."

"And thank you for doing business with God. We

91

know you have a choice of deities, and we're working hard to earn your satisfaction."

"Yeah, right. Okay."

I practiced being patient, but three more days passed and my soul mate still hadn't shown up. I called again, and noticed the same accent for the third time.

"Thank you for calling Heaven. My name is Suzan. How may I be of service?"

I spoke slowly while trying to put things together. "Hi, Suzan. How are you today?"

"I'm fine. Thank you for asking."

"I'm just curious. Are you one of my spirit guides?"

Long pause.

"Please hold. ... Thank you very much for holding. Yes, I work for God, from an off-site call center in order to serve you better. How may I help you?"

Off-site? How off-site? I wondered. Trying to sound friendly and non-threatening, I continued, "So where are you from, Suzan?"

"I am from the Planet Zgirdoo."

"Oh. How's the weather there?"

"It's a beautiful day. We're having a gas storm."

"Nice. Okay, well, I was just wondering where my soul mate is. I've been waiting a long time."

"I understand. Let me look up your account. Ah, yes, here it is. According to our records, you have to love yourself more."

"But my friend Jill has an adorable hunky

husband, and she's a mess. She hates herself! Why do I have to love myself first?"

"It is the lesson you chose for this lifetime."

"Do you say that to everyone who calls?"

"No. It is written right here in your akashic record, Mary, that your main lesson is to love yourself."

"I'm not Mary. I'm Marilyn. Marilyn Wilson, of 327 Elm Drive, Missouri City, Kansas."

"Please hold."

What's an Earthling to do?

The same thing you do with your computer: find an eleven-year-old. Kids already know this stuff. They don't have to be a Crystal or Indigo Child, a Starseed, or even in the gifted program. Any normal kid will do, as long as you didn't ruin her too much. That's what Marilyn did—she talked to her daughter, Summer Moonbeam. With the wisdom of innocence, Summer said, "Mom, we are so going shopping and getting you a vibrator."

Out of the mouths of babes.

Summer also helped Marilyn download some helpful videos.

EDITOR'S NOTE

Judging by the feedback we received, this column may have left readers with an overly negative impression of the Universe. Despite some problems with outsourcing, last year's survey showed customer satisfaction at 86%, beating earth's leader Apple Computer, which had its best year ever at 84%. It easily bested its old rival Satan, Inc., which scored a paltry 47% and had over twice as many unfavorable ratings.

The Universe had its best year in 361 A.D., when it was rated 98%. However, women and slaves were not allowed to participate in surveys then. Adjusted for that, its rating would have been about 91%. So even with today's more rigorous standards, the Universe is still earning high marks from most of its customers.

Despite that, God is trying to do better. In a recent interview, His spokesperson, Jesus H. Christ, said, "God takes customer satisfaction very seriously and is focused on improving the quality of our service. We've increased training at our call centers, and are committed to reducing long wait times and difficulties with consumers getting their questions answered."[1]

In addition, the Universe has a number of new programs aimed at increasing user-friendliness. For instance, on its recently redesigned website (http://theuniverse.com), there is a page where users can enter the name of any multi-level marketing company and calculate how much money and time they are likely to lose, as well as how rich they are likely to make the owner, before they give up. It can also calculate how much product they will still have in five-year increments in case they want to give it away

---

[1] This is from a Dell press release.

before the labels fall off. The Universe is betting that innovations like this will help push its numbers back into the 90s.

However, perhaps its biggest hurdle is in public relations. Christ took pains to point out that God does not control elections or the behavior of independent contractors such as priests. "Some of those who voted for Bush/Cheney later blamed us for them," he said, "although I think most of our customers understand that, by law, we are not permitted to vote. I should also mention that God has no power over bad cell phone coverage or exploding laptop batteries; we are strictly a spiritual company."

This year's ratings will be released next month.

PART VI

THE UNIVERSE

God is great. No, really, I mean that.
So are religions; they're all terrific.
Sure, they don't always agree.
No two people even agree on everything.
I hear God prefers it that way—
it keeps us on our toes
because we can never be totally sure we've got it right.

On your way to enlightenment,
you might want to take the best from each religion,
such as the parts about love and compassion.
However, whatever your religion,
or even if you don't have one,
the important thing is the Big Picture,
the Something that joins us all together.

I am a religious scholar, and in this chapter will take you
on a somewhat personal tour of the world's religions.

Here's a picture of me from 1998,
and one of Jesus from 26:

Chapter 26

THIS JUST IN FROM GOD:

THE SECOND COMING

You kids knock it off, or I'm coming down there mySelf!

QUEER EYE FOR THE OLD TESTAMENT DEITY

Nobody wears a white robe like God does, but his look could use some updating. I would start with shaving the beard—it ages him—and exfoliating. Tossing those lightning bolts is fine for His right bicep, but He needs a more balanced workout.

Also, He should cut down on burnt offerings; studies show that burnt foods are carcinogenic. The latest thing is raw, raw, raw! If He's going to eat red meat, it should be strictly grass-fed—at His age, grain-fed is too fatty.

He especially needs to try to eliminate the fatted calves. He, of all Deities, must know by now that veal is inhumane. I can't blame Him, though, if He has a weakness for veal scallopini—no One's perfect—but would it kill Him to ask for a chicken sacrifice once in a while?

I'm not saying He needs to go to the other extreme and adopt John the Baptist's locusts and honey diet, although it *is* raw. If He does, however, He should be sure to floss—locusts can become trapped between your teeth.

What is it with male deities and lightning bolts? Are they showing off? Do they think it makes them look macho? They need to set a better example. Maybe they should consider anger management classes.

I was a bit disappointed I wasn't chosen to be the new Pope. I never win anything! Being gay and Jewish might have been an issue, but John Paul II was Polish—I thought that opened the way.

I would have been a good Pope. There's a lot of dead wood in the Vatican—I'd have cleaned house. And redecorated; it's so dated! With all the gay priests around, you'd think it would have had a makeover by now.

Worse, what's with those hats? Hello! I would have appointed Phillip Treacy to the Holy See. He designs Kate Middleton's hats, and I'm sure he could do a bang-up job for the Pope and his cardinals. They need to set a better fashion example.

Being Jewish is much easier than being Catholic. You can get to Heaven just by marrying a doctor. The Internet has made it even more convenient: simply sign up at http://www.marryadoctor.com. I'm hoping for a cardiac surgeon.

We all know that God is Jewish, and of course, so was Jesus. There is evidence that Buddha was, as well; for one thing, he taught that life is suffering, which is exactly what my grandmother used to say. (Didn't anyone tell him about positive thinking?) He also clearly had a Jewish mother cooking for him; let's just say that he was in no danger of becoming a Weight Watchers spokesperson. Jesus only stayed so svelte because of all that walking—Mary's kugel was to die for.

Muhammad was also a nice Jewish boy. He did develop some problems at a certain point when his therapist took August off, but who hasn't?

VIRGIN TERRITORY

Islam is the world's fastest growing religion, perhaps because it offers men virgins in the afterlife. The Qur'an didn't mention the number of virgins awarded. However, after Muhammad's death, market researchers determined that seventy-two was the quantity needed to draw men away from sporting events.

Christianity also offers valuable perks, such as a seat at the right hand of God. Seats are available at the left hand of God, too, but they're not as good. Good seats have always done well in focus groups, which is why American Express also now offers them. In addition, Hinduism is giving frequent flyer miles to its reincarnating members, with no blackout dates.

Still, none of these programs come close to the

appeal of seventy-two virgins for straight men. Surprisingly, so far only Virgin Air is matching that offer. According to advertising agency Ogilvy & Mather, Christianity is going to have to sweeten its deal if it is to remain competitive. Creative director Ronald Smidley suggests offering 144 virgins of either or both genders to everyone. That would increase its appeal to modern women. "So far, none of the major religions have marketed extensively to women. However, as they gain equality, women are going to demand an equal number of hot virgins in Heaven." He also believes that such a policy would increase sales to the exploding LGBT demographic.

Islam's rapid growth is leading to severe virgin shortages and the issue of how to recycle them. Muslim men who aren't picky can instead get a thousand experienced *houris*, but there hasn't been much interest in this option. Smidley says that Islam will need to promote it heavily if the program is to continue, and that it could be a big success. One deceased Muslim, Saddam Gomorrah, who felt he couldn't handle seventy-two virgins, reported through the medium Nestor Caseworthy, "Those older *houris* sure know how to make a dead guy feel welcome."

Most of the world's 1.5 billion Muslims are upright, peace-loving citizens who vote on *Dancing with the Stars* and enjoy vampire/human romances. In fact, the Citizens Brigade for Truth is a nonpartisan coalition of

Muslims and Christians who are demanding that the government look into what really happened on *Lost*.

What we have in common is so much greater than our differences. Some of us may wear burqas, while others wear slutty clothes that expose our faces in public. Still, underneath our garb, we all have the same cottage cheese thighs that unite us in our humanity.

Recently, an Arab-American was crowned Miss USA. Rima Fakih, of Dearborn, Michigan, was born in Lebanon and raised in a Christian/Muslim household in New York. The lovely and talented Fakih won both the swimsuit and burqa competitions, bringing innocent sex appeal to each. Her ankle-length burqa by Israel Mizrahi was fuchsia silk lace over lilac satin, with a delicate floral niqab. Her lemon bikini by Armani Jihad was accented with lime tassels and minaret sunglasses. In her spare time, Ms. Fakih enjoys playing video games, pole dancing, and destroying infidels.

Perhaps Ms. Fakih will bring America together in ways that President Obama, whose story resembles hers, has not yet been able, although he is certainly equally hot in a swimsuit.

In a past life, I was Jesus's kid brother, Joe, Jr., of Nazareth. Once, he messaged me, "Hey, Joe, I'm going into the wilderness for forty days and forty nights. Could you help me move?" I adored him, but I hate moving, so I said no. Now I feel guilty. I'd like to make it up to him during the Second Coming by taking Him out for a terrific Last Supper at Peking Dragon. Jews love Chinese food, and there wasn't any good Chinese in Nazareth back then.

My favorite Jewish restaurant is Sophie's Deli. Its motto is "Eat, bubelah! Look how you look." It's famous for its huge pastrami sandwiches, and you get a rugelach misfortune cookie with your check. The other night, mine read, "Take an umbrella, or you'll catch pneumonia and die."

Even in this lifetime, I looked like Jesus before I cut my hair. People often stopped me on the street and asked, "Hey, aren't you the Son of God?" I always gave them my autograph.

Anyway, this sometimes brought up the issue of personal hygiene. One fan who saw my picture wrote me, "I think you look like a cute Jesus, but Jesus was probably smelly, so I hope you don't have bad hygiene." Here was my reply:

Our parents were poor and couldn't afford health insurance, so instead of being born at Beth Israel Sinai Hospital, in their sanitary maternity ward, Jesus had to be born in a barn. However, it was a relatively clean barn, with fresh hay in the manger. The sheep and cattle were considerate, and went outside to do their doody. At least they did after

Mary yelled at them between labor screams, "Don't $#*t in here, you morons! This is the Son of God being born!" Of course, we're all sons and daughters of God.

In any case, when we were growing up, we may not have had a fancy bathroom with marble counters and a JetStream spa, but every Friday before the Sabbath, the whole Christ family went to the public swimming hole, swam several laps, and took showers, using strictly kosher soap. As Jesus got older, he started jogging *on* the water, but he still always took a good shower afterward. He also flossed regularly, using long strands of goat intestinal lining.

So for that period, Jesus was considered quite clean. In fact, people would often say to Him, "Hey, Jesus, you don't smell too bad today!" Since most people stank, that was a high compliment.

But yes, times and standards have changed, and I am Immaculately clean. I shower at least five times a day and disinfect my hands after anyone touches them.

Families can push your buttons, even if you're the Saviour. One time after Jesus had left home, he came back to visit. Our mother started in on Him about how he shouldn't walk on the water in his new sandals, and he lost it. The sky turned dark, lightning flashed, and the earth shook. After a moment, Mary said, "This is how you talk to your mother?"

I'm not into holidays much, especially the religious ones—there's too much sitting on hard seats. My favorite one is Daylight Savings Time Day. I love light in the evenings.

I do, however, enjoy the Annunciation. It celebrates the Virgin Mary getting the news that she couldn't have vodka in her tomato juice because she was pregnant. Boy, was she pissed.

Harry Krishna, along with his lovely wife Sylvia, also started a religion that not many Westerners are familiar with. Of course, they were Jewish, too. A song written about him over five thousand years ago survives to this day: "Harry Krishna! Harry Krishna! Krishna Krishna! Harry Harry!" Just his name, over and over. It's not Sondheim, but it has stood the test of time.

Harry and Sylvia were from India, as were many other all-time spiritual greats. Today's Indian adepts carry on the tradition, miraculously manifesting things such as jewelry and *vibhuti*, ash with healing properties. My guru, Baba Ganoush, manifests eggplant dip that is quite tasty on pita bread. Personally, I like it better than vibhuti.

It's always inspiring to sit at the feet of my guru. For one thing, I'm really into feet. But for another, he's so full of wisdom.

One day, a fellow disciple, Ramameintheassananda, asked him, "Baba, why is it that everyone else has a better life than I do? Why don't I ever get what I want?"

He replied, "My son, God hates you. But get over it! This isn't a popularity contest." He explained that as with everyone else, there are people God likes, and people He doesn't. One shouldn't take it personally—it's His problem, not yours. It's like that book, *What God Thinks of Me is None of My Business.*

"In a past life, you were one of those Philistines God smote, and He resents it that you reincarnated—He thinks that people He smites should stay smitten. Then, you rub His nose in it by having good taste, like maybe he was wrong to smite you. Still, that's no reason not to be happy. The important things are to love yourself and give me all your money."

BREAKING NEWS! INVADING EXTRATERRESTRIALS CONVERT CHRISTIANS

THE VATICAN—Missionaries from the planet Xor, using advanced powers of mind control, converted the world's 2.1 billion Christians today to the worship of their messiah, Wim the Jujube. A spokesperson for the Xorans, Zeezah Zeezahdian, said, "It was fairly easy, since the religions are similar. For instance, Jujubeism's scripture tells the story of the Final Brunch, at the end of which Wim says to his followers, 'Suck on this starch- and gum-based hard candy in remembrance of me.'"

However, the Jujubes were unable to convert Christians to their missionary position, the Most Holy Configuration, since Xorans have eleven appendages and eighteen orifices.

There are those who believe that God is female. If that's the case, it would cast the Bible in a different light.

Once, when I was channeling the Mabel entity, someone asked, "Why did God demand animal sacrifices in the Old Testament?"

She replied, "God was on the Atkins Diet back then, and had a thing for barbecued ribs. Now She's a vegan, and is on this grilled-lemon-tofu-with-lightly-steamed-asparagus kick. Go figure. God's ways are mysterious." That would explain the recent increase in soy sacrifice.

Einstein was famously quoted, "God does not play dice with the universe." However, I asked God about that, and She said She does enjoy a good game of craps occasionally. "Nothing ventured, nothing gained," She is fond of saying.

The Other Side is the unseen dimension of life.
When you become enlightened,
you'll be amazed at how your awareness of it expands.

In this chapter I speak, for the first time,
about my near-death experience.

Chapter 27

THE OTHER SIDE

I was lying back and saw a bright white light. It said "Dentalease" on it. I wanted to go toward it, but then I sensed an enveloping presence. "It's not your time yet," the gentle, feminine voice said. "I'm not done cleaning your teeth." I shall never forget that.

In planning this lifetime, I originally wanted parents who were loving, healthy, spiritually conscious, emotionally mature, psychologically aware, artistically expressive, and financially secure. Unfortunately, the waiting list was seventeen thousand years.

PAST-LIFE REGRESSION

At first, I thought I was in a hot tub. Then I saw my hosts sharpening a knife too long for a turkey over a huge tray. There were no chips or dip, only salt. *I'm cooked!* I thought.

I told them, "For gosh sakes, at least taste me before putting salt on me!"

The next thing I knew, I was being born again to a young couple in Duluth.

I just finished an out-of-body stint guest hosting the popular game show, "You Bet Your Astral," in which dead people try to guess the former identities of other dead people. On my episode, we had Lao Tzu and Salome. They were shorter in person.

If you encounter a negative spiritual entity, just say, "Ha, ha, ha! Rubbish! You have no power here. Now begone before someone drops a house on you." It also wouldn't hurt to wear ruby slippers. Or glass slippers. Even bunny slippers.

People are funny—most would rather be young,
but in the hotly competitive world of enlightenment,
everyone wants to be as old a soul as possible.
Few consider the ramifications:
What happens when your soul wrinkles and sags?
How about when you forget what planet you're on?

Being an old soul isn't all it's cracked up to be.
Fortunately, you can become enlightened at any age.

Chapter 28

IT'S NOT EASY BEING AN OLD SOUL

The myth is that being an old soul is unending multidimensional bliss. To dispel that notion, here is my interview with Ron,[1] a soul who is even older than Old King Cole, but not quite as merry.

SHEPHERD:

So Ron, what's it like being such a laid-back old soul?

RON:

Complicated, man. For one thing, I have wives, husbands, and children in several cities. It's hard to get to them all. Even with my bilocation skills, I can only be in two places at once. That leaves ten (eleven?) others. It keeps getting more stressful, even when I try to take it easy and go with the flow—know what I mean?

The hardest thing is when I'm popping in and out of parallel universes. I get the kids' names wrong, and my GPS can't sort out the addresses—it displays error messages such as "Coordinates do not exist in this universe." Luckily, there are Super 8s in most of them. I've spent many a night hunched over next to the mini fridge trying to get on the Internet so I could figure out where I was. You wouldn't believe what they call

---

[1] Not his real name.

113

Google in some parallels (I can't repeat it here). Forget about your Frequent Sleeper points: they don't transfer to other universes. I've had several arguments about that with Hindu night clerks. Yes, they're Hindu in every universe. I don't know how that happened. It seems like it should violate some law of quantum physics.

Unfortunately, none of my wives or husbands understand me. Neither do any of my boyfriends or girlfriends. Or animals. I would have at least expected Fido (Pericles in several universes) to understand me, but no; he just looks at me oddly, farts, and walks away.

Not even the Tao understands me, but on the bright side, I'm expanding the Tao's horizons. If every phenomenon made sense to the Tao, why bother?

SHEPHERD:

What advice would you give to other elderly souls?

RON:

Be sure to pack a universal adapter for your portable electronic devices.

SHEPHERD:

What is the most important lesson you've learned in your billions of years of experience?

RON:

The problem isn't people's souls being young or old; it's people—they drive you crazy! On the plus side, you get to drive them crazy, too.

However, if that doesn't appeal to you, you might get a digital video recorder and watch them with closed captioning. Have your food delivered and left outside your door. Avoid social networking sites—there are people on them, and they might talk to you.

SHEPHERD:

Maybe you need to pace yourself.

RON:

You're right. The trouble is that, despite what Nancy Reagan says, it's not easy to say no. If someone asks me to marry him or her, I don't want to disappoint her or him. Also, I have enormous respect for the institution of marriage, and weddings are such happy occasions. Happiness is the important thing, don't you agree?

SHEPHERD:

I suppose so. But I thought that you became wiser as you got older.

RON:

There's always room for improvement, man. I'm going to work on this. I affirm that today, if someone asks me to get married, I will definitely turn him down (unless he's devilishly handsome, in which case it's not my fault).

I'm also going to have a t-shirt made that says "NO!" on it in big letters. If I don't want to say it, I can just pull up my sweatshirt. I'm a big believer in making fashion statements.

The Tao is the Ground of All Being,
and we're each planted in it.

An acquaintance of mine, Yyyyyyyyyy ("Doris"),
who blogs for Sparks.tao,
heard I was here and emailed me, asking,
"What's a nice unit of consciousness of the All-That-Is
like you doing on a planet like this?"
I told her my story:

Chapter 29

THE TAO TRAVEL AGENCY

I was browsing at the Tao Travel Agency, leafing through brochures describing the various games and watching 7-D simulations. I'd been thinking about taking some time off from my job in the Hole Generation department at Tao Power & Light. I'm a frequent flyer, having already taken sixteen trips into the dimensional universe. That's nothing compared to some, but it's all relative.

Of course, there are zillions of possible destinations, but you can't see them all, and it's hard to pick one. I sometimes take my buds' suggestions, which is how I ended up on Planet Slime; there's no accounting for taste, but every destination has its points.

I'd mostly ensouled on suburban planets and a few that were in the middle of nowhere. When you get right down to it, though, isn't every place in the middle of nowhere (which is also now here)? They're all just holographic constructs, playgrounds for our infinite mind. I'm not telling you anything you don't already know.

I'd been thinking about doing an urban trip this time, perhaps in the central solar system—something rad and ultra-high tech, maybe sixth dimensional. However, a blue-green planet in the boonies caught my eye. My agent, Aaaaaaeeeeeeee, an undulating ball of purple heat, came by. She had worked with me on my last five planetary adventures.

"Ah, Terra," she said. "That's an interesting one. It's among our trendiest destinations. It has a stunning variety of minerals, plants, and animals. Humanoid sentients there only come in two models, innie and outie, but there are some options and accessories. The dynamics within and between them are fascinating. Also, their hardwiring is aggressive, a nine on a scale of two to thirteen, so they will sometimes blow things up.

"Terra is attracting players with a wide range of experience, from newbies to those with as many as nineteen previous games, so that will mix things up a good deal. It should be one of the most unpredictable leagues in the semi-pros.

"The experiment there is about balance, so we've thrown together a large number of extremes. The goal of the game is to harmonize without any element losing its essential beingness."

"It sounds fun," I said.

"It is," she replied, "but it's not an easy place. You'd need to be prepared for a roller-coaster ride—wolves and lambs there won't be sharing beach condos anytime soon. However, you can improve your skills considerably and add much valuable knowledge to the banks.

"Terra has a preview function in deva mode, so if you're interested, just enter white hole W3R@\AX-19302>><<194Y7. If you don't like it, there's no obligation."

"I'll give it a try."

I got some buds together, and a few nnneeeny-nanos later, we were sliding down the chute, which is always a blast.

We were immediately impressed with Terra's beauty. I decided to hang out with the plant devas for several zzzeeeny-nanos. A few of my buds got a kick out of playing with the mammoth animal forms, while others were intrigued with the bacteria. Probably the most excitement was from riding erupting volcanoes. However, I was enchanted with the ravishing plant life.

Humans at that time were even more primitive, and rather ugly, if you ask me: semi-hairless, and their hygiene wasn't the greatest. But my buds and I agreed that this life form had real potential. For one thing, it was full of heart and desire. For another, it was a little crazy; I like that in a species.

Back at the Agency, Aaaaaaeeeeeeee was delighted with my decision to sign up for Terra. "You'll probably hate it sometimes, but in the end you'll be proud you took the challenge. If the inhabitants achieve balance, it could propel this universe forward significantly. The Tao will be watching with much interest."

A bunch of my buds and buds' buds got together to form a team and plan our strategy. I took a position that's intellectual yet creative, less kinesthetic than I was used to, which was a nice change of pace. Then, the Tao spit us out in groups of seven, because this universe is set up on a seven platform. I've always enjoyed seven universes.

It's been a terrific eighty thousand Terra years.

120

(Has it really been that many?) Yes, there have been ups and downs, but I can safely say that I'm not the same spark I was when I started. Travel changes you.

We're coming to the climax of phase I, and it's riveting. There are many beings coming into balance. To spice things up even more, new brainwave scramblers have been introduced. They have tongue-in-cheek names such as "news," "reality TV," and "customer service." Like most things here, they test our knowledge of truth and challenge us to transcend the illusion of differences. Will we claim our oneness and love all beings with compassion?

Sentients from other planets are crowding the bleachers. They're calling this the Game of the Xxxxxxxeeeny-nano, and the betting is fast and furious. My bet is on us—I think we can do this—but it's going to be close.

I'll give you an update in a nnneeeny-nano or two. If the whole thing blows, I'll be home early. Travel insurance can sure come in handy on a planet like this.

Signing off,
Qqqqqqqqqqqqqqqqaaaaha

PART VII

CHANGING THE WORLD

It's good to see the big picture,
but enlightenment begins at home,
and at the mall.

Chapter 30

WATCHES

Have you noticed the commercials before Christmas for extremely expensive watches? They don't mention prices, but they seem to say that if you truly love your special someone, you'll spend the kids' college money and get him or her a diamond-studded platinum waterproof watch. It doesn't matter if he leaves it at the gym; it's the thought that counts. It doesn't matter if she never scuba dives and, in fact, doesn't know how to swim. It doesn't matter if nowadays, $5 watches keep virtually perfect time. This is *love* we're talking about. Nothing says love like a 400% markup.

Some people think they haven't achieved legitimacy until they have an expensive watch. Also, some believe that $300 jeans are better than $30 jeans, that they'll get sick if they don't kill all household germs with toxic chemicals, and that a KFC bucket of drums and thighs will bring their family together.

Enlightenment is about consciousness. It's not how much you spend that matters, but whether you spend consciously, from your knowledge and wisdom. Something expensive may be worth it if you treasure it and it adds value to you life.

I did once splurge and buy a watch that cost eight times more than my previous ones—$40. It lasted three years, until I dropped it and all the glued-on numbers fell off. (It still worked, but it looked like a snow globe.) However, I didn't want to spend that kind of money again—the extra functions had turned out to be more trouble than they were worth. Still, life is too short to wear a clunky watch. I could have gotten another perfectly acceptable $5 watch, but I chose to spend $8. I'm worth $8, and I don't regret it one bit. Sometimes you have to spend another $3 at Walmart to get class and elegance. If you don't examine it too closely, you can't tell it's not a Rolex. And I don't expect you to, because it's just a watch. Why would you be staring at my wrist? Is that truly my most interesting feature? How about my dazzling smile? Hey, keep your eyes up here, buddy!

I'm a red-blooded American who firmly believes in shopping, the flag, and apple pie. If anyone speaks against apple pie, I will come to its defense, although it usually has too much sugar, and a sprouted whole grain crust would be more healthful. Also, I find rhubarb and cherry pies to be more interesting, but that's just me. And shouldn't there be a gluten-free alternative?

Furthermore, I adore the flag, although personally, I think it's time for an update: rose, cream, and periwinkle, for instance, would be more pleasant than those harsh primary colors.

And there's nothing like a patriotic trip to the mall. Spending money on expensive imported goods is what made our country great. However, if you just want to stimulate the economy, you could buy this book for your senator.

The enlightened find truth everywhere,
even in politics.

Chapter 31

POLITICS & NAKED SHOPPING

For years, readers begged me to run for president. Since Barack Obama was elected, that has died down a bit—people seem to feel he's almost as good as me, and frankly, he has better abs. Still, I will not ignore the cries of the little people (five foot three and under), and reserve the right to jump in the race any time, even if there isn't one.

However, let me make one thing perfectly clear: I shall not, under any circumstance, wear a tie. I hate ties, and besides, you don't see any hot movie stars wearing them, do you? It's time for change.

I can hear Rush Limbaugh saying, "There, he's gone and done it—he's desecrated everything we hold dear. First European watches, then designer jeans, household disinfectants, KFC, and now ties, for chrissakes! And he wants to change the recipe for apple pie. Is nothing sacred? The next thing you know, he'll be advocating naked shopping! Our malls will be filled with naked people if he's elected!"

Now that you mention it, Rush, people shopped naked for thousands of years. Shopping naked is an inalienable right. We already have the right to bear arms. What about our right to bare butts? I will defend to the death our right to shop naked.

(Rush becomes apoplectic.) "If he becomes president, life as we know it will disintegrate and cease to exist!"

And that would be bad because ...?

Nakedness is not only our right but our sacred duty in the fight against terrorism. If people removed their clothes before going into public places, it would keep potentially lethal bombs, liquid cosmetics, and toenail clippers out of our office buildings, malls, buses, and airplanes. As a side benefit, it would make C-SPAN and press conferences more interesting, and it would eliminate tweets from Congressmen in their underwear.

Some male terrorists belong to a religion that forbids them from looking on women other than their wives. The San Onofre Nuclear Generating Station in Southern California has been spared a terrorist attack because it's on a nude beach and its reactors look like breasts (see photo). Women! Go topless for America!

It is also our duty to promote gay marriage, because it drives terrorists crazy. We should especially push it in Afghanistan. Marriage creates stability, and Afghanistan could use some gentrification. I propose that we offer a $50 gift certificate for the Kabul Linens 'n Stuff to every gay couple there who gets married, plus an additional $25 if they're also Sunni/Shiite. That would go a long way there, and even further with the 20% off coupon.

I'm a uniter, not a divider.
This is not a country of Democrats,
Republicans, and Nakedists, but of Americans!
Enlightenment is about unconditional love.

Still, as much as I try to reach out
and touch someone across the aisle,
I pull back.
I can love them in the abstract,
but could I ever be *in* love with a Republican?

Chapter 32

SOUL MATES?

My soul and personality had an interesting conversation the other morning while I was in the tub. Here's a transcript of it from the akashic records:

SOUL: What would you think if I was able to finally bring you the mate you've always wanted, only he was a Republican?

PERSONALITY: Should I slit my wrists now or wait until after we move in together? ...

Would he be cute?

S: Yes.

P: Could we just agree never to talk about politics?

S: No.

P: Don't you think we have enough tests on the physical plane without going out of our way?

S: (No answer.)

P: At least he'd be rich and have a nice car, right?

S: It's not bad.

P: He's not a fundie, is he? I would definitely draw the line at that.

S: No. He's a new ager.

P: Really?
Isn't there anyone else out there for me? Maybe a hot anarchist? How about a Green Party member with dimples?

S: Not at the moment.

P: What about an apolitical dwarf with a speech impediment? ...
You know, some of my best friends are Republicans. Actually, one of my best friends *dated* a Republican (he's serving time now).
It could be sort of romantic: star-crossed lovers, like *Romeo and Julio*:

Two households, both alike in dignity,
In fair Verona Beach,

But isn't that a bit much? I'm not a drama queen.

S: (Looks down his glasses.)

P: So is this a rhetorical question?

S: There's someone I'd like you to meet.

BODY: (Swallows bath water.)

P: (Feverishly affirming.) "Different points of view make for a vital democracy. We can all work together for the common good. Dick Cheney is sometimes nice to dogs. Bill O'Reilly practices good dental hygiene. I love Republicans!"

The truth sets you free, and facts are local truths.
Verifying them is good practice for enlightenment.

Here, we delve into one of the issues in the news.

Chapter 33

FARMER IN DELL:
LIPSTICK ON PIG SPLOTCHES

ELL, IOWA—Politicians are always talking about putting lipstick on a pig, but is it possible? We decided to find out.

Most people assume that it is, due to the popular Muppets star Miss Piggy, who is never seen in public without being fully made up. However, we interviewed several witnesses who alleged that she is a puppet. Producers of Sesame Street did not return phone calls asking for comment.

We sent a reporter out into the field, or more precisely, the sty, belonging to farmer John Smith in Dell, Iowa. Smith borrowed his wife's tube of Mary Jay ApocaLips ("Have lips to die for! Your kisses will be the living end!! For women, too") in her favorite shade, Swollen Glands. He approached his sow Emily, whom he considered to be among his loveliest and, certainly, his most cooperative.

Emily appeared to enjoy the attention. However, Smith encountered a problem he compared to that of a drag queen putting foundation over a bad case of five o'clock shadow: pig lips are bristly, and even a heavy layer of lipstick looked splotchy; it was hard to get an even sheen.

As a test, we left Emily with a boar, Sam, who seemed indifferent to her new look, even when, according to psychic animal communicator Sylvia

Swatchmore, she asked, "Do you notice something different about me?" At first, Sam thought it was her hair, then wandered off when he heard some slop being served.

Smith's conclusion was that you can, indeed, put lipstick on a pig, but it's not a good look, unless you combine it with heels and a tasteful string of pearls. That, of course, is Miss Piggy's signature, for good reason, according to Smith. "The classics never go out of style," he maintained.

Will Farmer John try lipstick on other barnyard animals? "Probably not," he said, "but Bessie has beautiful dark eyes that might be highlighted with mascara and liner."

Enlightenment brings freedom.
Until then, everyone has a different idea what it is.

Chapter 34

HEALTHCARE & SOCIALISM

Dear Editor,

I am a concerned citizen who loves this country so much that I want to secede from it. The reason: I'm sick and tired of socialism. It is creeping into every part of American life. Healthcare is only the latest. The world was much better off when the government stayed out of people's business.

For instance, socialism has taken over education. Why is the government spending *my* money to educate other people's children? Public education never did me any good. If people want to have kids, they should educate them themselves. Why does everyone need to be able to read, anyway? How hard is it to turn on a television? You just click the biggest button on the remote.

Socialists are always crying about helping the poor. What about helping corporations, who do so much more for us? For instance, if it weren't for big corporations, we wouldn't have Chili Cheese Fritos. Clearly, big corporations are way better than big government.

Obama, who's not even a citizen, wants to socialize our roads. Big government, keep away from my Interstate Highway System! I like it fine just the way it is. In fact, I don't need roads at all—I have a two-ton four wheeler; I'll drive anywhere I damn well please. I don't need your stimulus package, either.

Mine is plenty big. At least, the ladies don't complain.

The government can't do anything right, like those levees in New Orleans that broke. President Bush was right not to throw good money after bad by trying to fix them. I don't even want the government pumping my drinking water and then charging me for it—I can pump my own. And what do we need with fancy government sewage systems? If pansy-kneed liberals don't like the smell of sewage flowing through the streets, they need to toughen up.

Also, why are my tax dollars being spent on libraries for books about homosexuals and farm animal fornicators? They can buy their own books—there are sections for them in every adult bookstore.

I'm especially angry about socialized defense. Before big government, if people wanted to invade another country, they practiced self-reliance and did it themselves. They'd get a bunch of guys together and a few "spears 'n beers." They'd hike however far it was, ride a horse, or mush a dog sled, and attack. It was good exercise, except for those who got killed, and they didn't need any new-fangled equipment. Today, people have gotten soft and rely on government welfare for the military-industrial complex.

I admit it's a bit harder to invade a Middle Eastern country than the next town, but if the government didn't interfere, the free market would do its magic and things would work fine. For example, let's say that a bunch of manly men in Rochester wanted to invade Jordan. They could get bids from different airlines and find the best price for transporting them to Amman. I'll bet the winner would even throw in, at no extra charge, dropping a few bombs along the way. Competition and privatization always work. Or my buddies at Halliburton will give you a deal.

Our defense budget is over $660 billion. My share of that is at least $2000. I could definitely spend it better than the government. For two grand, I could buy a professional-grade assault rifle to take to town hall meetings and enough ammo to last several weeks. The Founding Fathers wanted us to form our own militias. I say to big government: take your sticky mitts off my military. Let me be free!

If people get sick, why should the government bail them out? Survival of the fittest—that's God's way. I don't rely on government handouts; I go to the VA hospital. If people starve themselves and get sick, they should take responsibility and eat.

In the old days, governments just provided necessary services, like removing corpses from the streets. I'm willing to pay for that. But we've got to stop socialism before it's too late and everyone has healthcare with death panels, like those snooty Brits who think they're better than us but are worse than the French when they opposed the liberation of Iraq.

As a proud American, I'm happy to stand guard against the Russians from my porch, but those Brits have invaded us twice before, and I wouldn't put it past them to try it again. Don't count on big government to stop them—Obama's in bed with the

Queen—and I can't do it all myself. We have to work together to stand up to the march of socialism. Gentlemen, man your Hummers and load your rifles! They'll give me universal healthcare over my dead body.

Sincerely,
Todd P.
Wasilla, Alaska

The online world (is there any other?)
reflects the pushes and pulls of all human relationships,
our need for space battling our desire
to make ourselves known,
and our insecurities making us a little nuts.

Chapter 35

LURKERS' RIGHTS

I'm a member of the Michael Teachings Yahoo! Group,[1] an email list that discusses a fascinating body of material about how we set up our lifetimes. The guidelines, written by moderator Jack,[2] are posted monthly. One of them encourages people to participate, not just "lurk."

One new list member interpreted this as unwelcoming and "subtle intimidation." She mistakenly remembered me as having sent her the guidelines. Another member, Jerry,[2] concurred, adding that he had greeted the "anti-lurker" comment with "disdain."

I include this dialogue here because of the important points it makes about democracy.

JERRY:

I have no tolerance or respect for rules. I have responded to the latest batch of political tongue-wagging on this list with silence, which I guess qualifies as lurking, a no-no according to the rules. #*@k that $&*t. I say what I want, when I want. I'll take my chances.[3]

---

[1] http://groups.yahoo.com/group/MichaelTeachings
[2] Not his real name.
[3] I am not making this up. In fact, I am not making up a surprising amount of this book.

SHEPHERD:

First, let me say that I've always been a staunch supporter of lurkers' rights. Others can vouch for my years of service as a volunteer with the Los Angeles chapter of the Lurkers' Anti-defamation League of America (LALALA). We believe that lurking is a valid alternative lifestyle and is constitutionally protected.

Yes, there are bigots who equate lurking with stalking, but I think we all know that's a right-wing fabrication. Lurkers are part of what makes this country great. "Motherhood, baseball, and lurking," I always say. In fact, I don't think the Internet could exist without lurkers—that's how important they are. If all list members posted every day, chaos would ensue—the whole system would break down. Your two posts certainly illustrate well the value of lurking.

Second, I do not follow guidelines of any kind. If there's a sign asking people not to pee on the toilet seat, I do it just to assert my right as an American— this is a free country, dammit! Nobody is going to tell me what to do.

I did read the guidelines after your posts, though, and the only thing I could find was "Talk. Please do not lurk. We are a very supportive group." Is that what you're referring to? Even as a member of LALALA, all I see there is an encouragement to participate, cheerleading by the moderator. As much as I support lurking (I often do it myself) and avoid doing anything in moderation, moderators have a right to cheerlead. (I'm getting an image of Jack shaking pompoms and wearing a short skirt with high-top Keds. Jack, please shave your legs if you're going to cheerlead in my head, for gosh sakes!)

If everyone lurked, there would be no list. Encouraging posting is part of Internet ecology, just like lurking. (Ecology: if there were no wolves, there would be too many little girls with red hoods. Balance must be maintained. Yin/yang. Dark/light. Lurk/post.)

Nowhere did Jack say, "Lurkers are the disgusting perverted scum of the earth and don't deserve the air they breathe let alone the bandwidth they take away from starving children in Africa who can't afford Internet access but who would certainly post if they had the opportunity." Or even, "Members who violate the 'no lurking' rule shall be banned." No, he just said, "Talk. Please do not lurk." Saying "please" demonstrated what an easy-going guy he is. I don't think he will be coming to your house anytime soon and pinning you down in front of your computer until you write a post. Besides, he's too busy, and he probably doesn't have your address. On the other hand, I wouldn't take chances.

I'm sure I'll get some flames from politically correct lurkers who see any defense of posters as an incursion on lurkers' rights. *Bring 'em on!* to quote another famous macho guy. 'Cause if you post, you're no longer a lurker. Got you there.

145

There's a Zen saying,
"Before enlightenment, chop wood, carry water;
after enlightenment, chop wood, carry water."
Apparently, Wu Li didn't have
central heating and indoor plumbing.

However, the point is that ordinary things are important—
enlightened people don't reject them,
but instead infuse them with light.

If Wu were alive today, he might say,
"After enlightenment, floss."

Chapter 36

PHILANTHROPY

My many philanthropic efforts include the much-heralded Homeless Flossing Project.

A recent study showed that a shocking 88% of homeless people do not floss. During the brutally cold winter months, this figure rises to 94%. Of course, this bodes disastrously for their long-term dental health. Therefore, I formed the HFP in 2007 to combat this epidemic.

In the Project's pilot cities, Cleveland, Baltimore, Fargo, and Miami Beach, whenever temperatures drop below thirty-two degrees, volunteers hit the streets in specially designed FlossMobiles. The floss is acquired through the generous support of organizations such as the American Society for Dental Hygiene and the U.S. Department of Health and Human Service's Floss Surplus Subsidy program.

When a homeless person is found freezing on the street, a team of two volunteers greets him and offers him a roll of floss. The first is a trained flossing demonstrator who shows him proper technique. For example, we emphasize the vital importance of using a clean section for each tooth. Education is our number one goal—if we can help our clients understand that plaque is their enemy, we will have done our job. The second team member is trained in martial arts in case the homeless person attempts to strangle the flossing demonstrator with his floss.

In just four years, with an annual budget of under $45 million, we have seen a drop in flosslessness in our target demographic of over .05%. In recognition of our accomplishments, I received the Medal of Freedom from President Bush in 2008. One person *can* make a difference.

PART VIII

THE CREATIVE ARTS

Shakespeare showed us that enlightened people
aren't necessarily crummy writers.
(Transcending the mind is all well and good,
but you can take that a bit too far.)

In a past life, I was Shakespeare's third cousin
and inspiration for Hunchback Dick.
I like to think I learned a thing or two.

Here are some modest stabs
at an enlightened literary style:

Chapter 37

LITERATURE

It was a dark and stormy night. Well, nights *are* dark, by definition, especially when they're stormy, and this one was no exception. Though, in fact, some nights aren't dark, especially in the far north during the summer. But then, are they nights if the sun hasn't set? And nights aren't that dark if there are street lamps, or the moon is full. However, if you can't read a Kindle outside, it's still dark, in my book. I don't want to argue about this anymore.

It was a clear and sunny afternoon.

Her life was as carefree as a tampon commercial.

Being a shrewd businessman, he leased his soul to the devil.

She went into a trance and was never seen again.

As a holistic efficiency expert, he always tried to heal two birds with one herb.

You permeate my heart like organic eggs in whole-grain French toast, like dust mites in my mattress, like Glade Apricot Morning in my coat closet.

I long for your laughter, which sparkles in my memory like Blue Light Specials at K-Mart.

I find it hard to live without you, but I know I must, for you would want me to be brave. So I put on a happy face, as in the Broadway musical *Bye Bye Birdie*, but inside, my heart is as empty as my colon after a wheatgrass colonic, and my liver, drier and tougher than the liver special at Denny's.

His positive, upbeat attitude allowed him to thoroughly enjoy the breathtaking scenery on the road to ruin. "We got good weather, too!" he exclaimed, with a Pepsodent smile.

Winnifred Sludgemouth was as shy and genteel as a feather. It dismayed her to no end that people assumed she was crass and loud. "You should never judge a fictional character by her name," she'd often gently admonish readers.

Being the wild and quiet guy he was, he felt a need to sow his Quaker Oats.

If her heart were any bigger, she wouldn't have room for her lungs and kidneys.

He had places to go, people to do.

She was as happy as a fly swimming in a bowl of melting Haagen-Dazs.

That feisty television chef was full of piss and vinaigrette.

Despite her family being a little dysfunctional, it was good to be home again. The birds were mooing, the cows were singing, and the sun was blue.

She had that new car smell.

His heart was in the right place, but his head was so far up his *ss he could see his tonsils.

He moved like an animal: he had the grace of a rat, the tightly coiled reflexes of a moose, and the cunning of a poodle.

Everything has consciousness.
When you're enlightened,
you'll be able to communicate easily
with all other beings, including animals,
just like Doctor Doolittle.

This is one of many things movies teach us.

Chapter 38

AT THE MOVIES

It was synchronous that *King Kong* and *The Chronicles of Narnia: The Lion, the Witch and the Wardrobe*, two important films starring animals, were released at the same time.

I'd heard earlier that *Kong's* director, Peter Jackson, had been planning to update the story and have Kong fall for Adrien Brody, a sort of cross-species *Brokeback Island*, but Brody wasn't available. They had also considered retitling it *Queen Kong*, featuring a gorilla transvestite, but in tests, his tutu kept falling off. At least, it was fortunate that Jackson was able to get Andy Serkis to play Kong, since it's always hard to find someone twenty-five feet tall who can act.

Incidentally, after years of actors and models shaving their chests, *Kong* began a trend, and hairy males are now back in vogue. Ann Darrow's line when she was nestled in Kong's arm, "Oh, you big hairy ape!" became a catchphrase.

Although *King Kong* is primarily an action movie, it is also an eloquent plea for tolerance of interspecies marriage, which is currently banned in over thirty states. For example, in California, it is still illegal to marry your dog! It doesn't matter how long you've been together or how faithful he is. It's true that dogs sometimes stray, but they are generally wonderful partners.

Narnia is a retelling of the New Testament, with

Aslan, a lion, standing in for Jesus. In some ways, it surpasses the original. For instance, in *Narnia*, many people were raised from the dead, versus just one, Lazarus, by Jesus. Furthermore, kids got to be in charge in *Narnia*; there were no major child characters in the Jesus story, and only two animals, a camel and a donkey—neither were speaking roles.

Although Peter Jackson directed *Kong* and not *Narnia*, *Narnia* is reminiscent of his *Lord of the Rings* in its tale of elemental beings in another dimension, and the battle between good and evil. I'm happy to report that, once again, good triumphed over evil. Let that be a lesson to all evil-doers. Now, if we could just convince them that they're evil, we'd have it made: we could show them movies like this and they'd realize that evil doesn't pay. Unfortunately, they seem to think the evil ones are those other people over there, or even us! I guess we're just going to have to keep killing them until they get it.

In many movies, much of the excitement comes from characters being chased, often by animals. That invokes our primal memories of trying to outrun them so as to avoid being dinner. Personally, I find all that adrenalin wearing—I get plenty just trying to balance my checkbook.

Avatar is another inspiring film about respecting people's rights and killing those who don't. It awakened in many a longing for a lost paradise; not in me, though. As beautiful as Pandora was, I'm afraid of heights and don't run fast—it was full of wild animals! The Na'vi had good relations with them, but look what happened to Siegfried and Roy. Even worse, Pandora had no Whole Foods, HDTV, *or* massage loungers. Just think: if you lived on Pandora, you would not be able to rent *Avatar*.

However, they're building a magnificent gated resort, so I hope to take a vacation there someday.

THE BOY FROM MARS

I have a meeting with Spielberg next week to pitch a movie with me starring as a rascally planet-hopping miner (sort of a young Harrison Ford) who falls in love with a red (and red-hot) atavistic Martian man who's three feet tall.

Besides it being a musical, the main difference between it and *Avatar* is that Mars isn't very attractive, and we have enormous fun blowing it up. My home planet has a desperate shortage of land-scaping gravel, and red rock is especially prized. Hopefully, this movie will remind people how married gay interplanetary couples can improve their neighborhood through harmonious landscape architecture memorializing the great planet Mars once was.

Theater is one of our oldest art forms,
dating back almost ninety thousand years,
when the first caveboy next door
said to his girlfriend, Judy,
"Ugh! We put on show!"

Enlightened people create by using
the power of their imagination
to see things that don't yet exist,
which is also what theater people do.

Chapter 39

THEATER NEWS

LOW-BUDGET SONDHEIM FESTIVAL OFFERS THREE-FOR-ONE

TALLAHASSEE, FLORIDA—Many creative theater companies have found ways to plumb the depths of the legendary musical theater composer-lyricist Stephen Sondheim on a shoestring. The always cutting-edge Swamp Theatre Workshop in Tallahassee, Florida, is debuting an annual Sondheim festival that will combine two or more of his musicals into one. The first offering will be the *Gypsy Todd Follies*, about a psychopathic stage mother who fries producers in chow mein when they won't cast her daughters. The big number is "Have an Egg Roll, Mr. Weismann."

Coming next year will be *A Little Evening Primrose*, in which the Liebesliebers wordlessly waltz once too often and, in the finale, are silently displayed taxidermied against the stunning northern lights.

THE SOUND OF MUSIC "REVISAL" OFFERS EXCITING NEW TAKE ON FAMILIAR MATERIAL

LONDON—Classic American musicals such as *Cabaret* and *Carousel* have been rethought for today by brilliant British directors, revealing depth and meaning that had been covered over by years of rote productions. Raymond Longbottom, founder of the prestigious

Grunge Warehouse, may have a new groundbreaking hit on his hands with his staging of *The Sound of Music*.

Although the stage version was eclipsed by the film, the most successful movie musical of all time, it contains "much heretofore untapped subtext and genuine, unsentimental feeling," said Longbottom. Here is an outline of his upcoming all-star production:

Maria is a real handful at the Abbey. She breaks into show tunes at the drop of a hat. When Sister Josephina Margaretha (Judith Ivy) accidentally walks in on her when she is bathing, it is discovered that Maria (John Cameron Mitchell) is a drag queen ("How Do You Solve a Problem Like Maria?"). She is sent to work as a maid for Captain von Trapp (Richard Chamberlain) to give her some much-needed discipline ("Do-Re Me!"), where she discovers his dungeon ("My Favorite Things"). However, soon she has made curtains for it out of the children's old play clothes, and has turned it into a fashionable piano bar ("The Sound of Music"). There, the Captain meets millionairess Elsa (Charles Busch), who puts the make on him, along with everything else that moves ("The Lonely Goatherd").

Of course, the children want to stay up late and attend the midnight show, so Maria teaches them a song ("So Long! Farewell!! Shut Up Already!!!"). Unfortunately, they can't carry a tune in a bucket, but they sing it anyway, and everybody claps politely. When the Captain sees how Maria encourages his tone-deaf children, he realizes he's falling in love with her. Maria has a fear of commitment due to having been sexually abused by her father, five uncles, and the Austrian 16th Regiment ("Sixteen Going on Seventeen"), and she runs away back to the Abbey. Mother Superior (Whoopi Goldberg) tells her to get the hell out of there and suggests that she walk to Switzerland, where she can have an operation (the inspiring "Climb Every Mountain"). However, Maria hates exercise and decides to go back to the Captain, where he wins her over in the dungeon. They decide to marry, but by now, the Nazis have marched in and banned gay marriage.

Meanwhile, the Captain's daughter Liesl (Lindsay Lohan) discovers that her boyfriend Rolf (Zac Efron) has joined Hitler Youth. However, since he made her do it on the grass ("Edelweiss") with her best friend Marlene (Paris Hilton), she doesn't care anymore. Maria helps her realize that she's a lesbian ("No Way to Stop It").

Elsa's friend Max (Anthony Hopkins) organizes gay cruises, and offers the Captain a discount for his family if they'll create a dungeon piano bar onboard (reprise, "The Sound of Music"). After much begging, the Captain agrees. However, the Nazis take over Capri and their other destinations, and threaten them with exorbitant duty taxes on linen, crystal, and fine wine. He safely pilots the ship to Vermont, where he and Maria marry and start a chain of fabulous piano bars (reprise, "Climb Every Mountain").

Poetry was also invented by cavepersons.
When everything you write has to be carved in stone,
you learn to chose words economically.
The first poem, from 52,000 BCE,
was by a poet known as the Ogster:

CARCASS ROTTING
MAGGOTS CRAWLING
FLIES FLYING
YUM

(Archeologists recently learned that the Ogster
was a woman writing under a male pseudonym.)

Chapter 40

POETRY SLAMMED

LIMERICK

He searched but he couldn't get nearer.
He'd lost himself in the mirror.
He looked high and low
But wherever he'd go,
Nowhere was he there
To be here.

IF I WERE DISCIPLINED

If I were disciplined,
I would have abs,
A waist,
And buns of steel.

If I were disciplined,
I would go to bed every night at ten
And get up early every morning.
I would not waste time.
I would be efficient.
My days would be packed
With productivity.
I would be five minutes early for everything
Rather than five minutes late.

If I were disciplined,
I would read only articles
That bettered me.
I would not read about actors,
The latest computers,
Or zillion-dollar houses.
I would read all the books I buy,
And do all the projects I buy them for.

If I were disciplined,
I would meditate every day
And would probably be enlightened by now.
I would do yoga
And be able to touch my ears
With my toes,
Which might come in handy sometime.

If I were disciplined,
I would not eat sugar,
Or snack after dinner.
I would eat mostly leafy greens
And rare lean meats
Without barbecue sauce.
My body fat
Would be negative three percent.

If I were disciplined,
I would be a piano virtuoso,
And people would be very impressed.
I would create great works of art
And not poems like this.

If I were disciplined,
I would write a book every year.
I would not read and write email all day.
I would brush after every meal,
And have a musical on Broadway.

If I were disciplined,
I would be concise,
To the point,
Terse,
Succinct,
Pithy,
Incisive,
Brief.

If I were disciplined,
I would save the world.
I would make myself do
All the things I don't want to do
To accomplish the things I want to.
Or, I could just
Do the things I like to do
For the love of doing them,
But would that be cheating?

If I were disciplined,
I would at least finish this poem,
But

When I'm not writing
bestselling books about enlightenment,
I sometimes write show tunes.
Here are three of my lyrics.[1]

Chapter 41

LYRICS

FALL IN LOVE

Verse:

I tell you that I like you a lot.
You sit there smiling,
Looking so beguiling,
But you don't say a word,
Not a blessed word.

And now my head is feeling so hot.
I'm getting thinner,
Picking at my dinner
Like a little bird.

Love birds are in season
And I'm a sitting duck,
Without any reason
To hope for luck.

So may I give a penny for your thought?
Make that a twenty.
Here, I've got plenty,
But don't be noncommittal.
Please don't be noncommittal.

Since I met you, I'm so overwrought.
Please say that maybe
You'll want my baby,
Or just encourage me a little.

Lover's Leap has danger,
And I won't jump alone.
I'm not the Lone Ranger
Who likes it on his own.

I'm on the cliff
Waiting to know if
You would like to fall in love with me.
'Cause

Refrain:

I could easily fall in love,
Fall in love with you.
I could easily fall in love
If you wanted me to.

My heart is fluttering in my chest,
Jumping all around.
If you told me you like me best,
It would really start to pound.

These anti-gravity shoes
Are giving me the blues.
They make me walk on the air,
So what are you doing down there?

I'd run the gamut from A to Z
In ten seconds flat.
Sadly here I am stuck at B,
Wondering where you're at.

I would gladly jump off my bed,
Flap my arms and fly,
Joining the tweety birds 'round my head,
If I had a reason why.

I could go nuts very soon.
Oh, God, there's a full moon!
I stay up nights counting sheep
So why are you able to sleep?

I could easily fall in love,
Fall in love with you.
I could easily fall in love,
Fall in love, fall in love.

I could easily fall in love,
Fall in love, fall in love.
I could easily fall in love,
Fall in love, fall in love.

If you wanted me,
If you wanted me,
If you wanted me to.

A LITTLE SINNING

Verse:

When you've been good,
Just as good as can be,
Done what you should,
Everything from A to Z,

(You've not touched pot or booze
Or sex or cards,
Or any other nasty things.
In a day or two,
You'd have sprouted wings.)

But then you feel
Like you're going to burst.
You must conceal
Your desire to do your worst.

If you just let it out
A bit at a time,
You'll be so very awf'ly glad.
How good it is
To be a little bit bad.

Refrain:

For we need a little sinning
To chase the blues away.
Just a little sinning
To brighten up each day.

It's amazing what some naughty words will do.
They can change your cloudy skies of gray
To skies of blue—
Just one or two.

You
Need a little sinning
To see you never frown.
Just a little sinning,
So keep your sunny side down.

Yes, we need a little sinning to be carefree.
Just a little sinning,
Just a little sinning,
Just a little sinning
For you and me.

A COUNTRY-WESTERN SONG

My life is full of trouble.
My pillow every night is wet, son.
I'm in love with Betty Rubble,
But I'm stuck with Jane Jetson.
All I want is an old-faaaaaaaashioned girl.

PART IX

BUT ENOUGH
ABOUT YOU

By this time, dear reader, you no doubt have started to think of me as a good friend. You have already searched the Internet for naked pictures of me (which I can certainly understand). Yes, we've bonded through these pages, and now you want to know more about me.

Birth and death are the bookends of life. Birth itself involves disgusting body fluids, so let's not discuss that. However, birthdays are occasions that can help you examine your life, as well as get free stuff. Perhaps an exploration of my birthdays will give you some insight into who I am.

This is a photo of me taken shortly before I gave up white flour and sugar in my quest for enlightenment.

Chapter 42

BIRTHDAYS

'm going to be celebrating my 30th birthday. It was in 1984, but it was too traumatic to celebrate then. I think I can now truly accept turning 30.

I don't know when I'll feel ready to celebrate my 40th. I've been making progress with my new therapist, so maybe in another few years.

SOME FRIENDS SENT ME THIS

For your birthday, we've arranged a little New York City vacation. Here's the itinerary:

7:30–8:30 a.m.: Breakfast at Gracie Mansion with Rudy, Ed, and the current mayor what's-his-name. Advise on rebuilding lower Manhattan already.

9 a.m.–noon: Address the U.N. General Assembly on your plan for world peace.

12:30–1:30 p.m.: Lunch at Le Cirque with Robin, Whoopi, and Billy. Ad lib some material for the next *Comic Relief*. Give them the screenplay you've written for them, a remake of *The Three Stooges*.

2–4:45 p.m.: Fill in for the lead at the matinee of your choice:

a) *Phantom of the Opera*
b) *Billy Elliot,* or
c) *Wicked*

5:00–5:20 p.m.: Beauty rest back at the Plaza.

5:30–6:00 p.m.: Cocktails with Woody and Stephen. Help Stephen write his next project, a musical of *Schindler's List.* Film a cameo for Woody's current film in which he plays an aging neurotic Jewish man who marries a supermodel.

6:30–7:30 p.m.: Dinner at Mario's in Queens with the Yankees and Mets celebrating your birthday and commemorating your contributions to baseball.

8–10:00 p.m.: Concert at Madison Square Garden performing your original songs with your choice of back-up singers:

a) Barbra Streisand
b) The Rolling Stones
c) Plácido Domingo
d) Justin Bieber, or
e) All of the above

10:30–11:00 p.m.: Guest appearance on *Late Night with David Letterman.* Present the Top Ten Reasons Channels Make the Best Lovers.

11:30 p.m.–12 a.m.: Ice cream and cake at the top of the Empire State Building with the president, members of the cabinet, Congress, and the Supreme Court, who chartered a special party train from Washington.

NOTE: I ended up having to spread this out over two days.

The president was going to honor me with a national holiday. However, I asked him not to; I like getting mail on my birthday.

In my twenty-eight odd years of life (the other twenty-eight were even), I've learned the power of affirmations. Since I passed my most recent milestone (and gallstone), I've been affirming: "The older, fatter, and balder I become, the better looking I am."

Here are some birthday greetings for the cynic in your life:

• "A loving wish that this special day suck less than usual."

• "Hoping that all the a-holes you meet have rosewater enemas."

• "When your life goes down the drain, may the pipes be clogged."

I know that this chapter
is why you bought the book.
You will not be disappointed.

Chapter 43

MY LOVE LIFE

Everyone has a favorite compliment, such as "You look nice today" or "You handled that well." Mine is "You are the sexiest hunk I've ever seen in my entire life. Yet you are much more than just an extraordinarily good looking sex object: you are a brilliant theoretical mathematician and anthropologist, a marvelously inventive and sympathetic bartender, a dazzling soccer player and ballet dancer, and a heck of a nice guy to boot." My second favorite compliment is "Your breath is minty fresh."

Someone asked me, "Why can't everybody be like you?" I explained that if too many people were as hot as I am, it would increase global warming and we'd all drown.

I had a difficult loss. *People* magazine came out with their Sexiest Man Alive issue, and once again, I was passed over. I wasn't even one of the hundred runners-up. They had several consolation prize categories, too, like Sexiest Hottie Under Four Feet Tall and Sexiest Man with Ingrown Toenails; they could have at least made a category for me.

I felt better, though, when I was named "Sexiest Man Alive or Dead" by *Astral Plane* magazine. It was such an honor, especially when there are so many dead people more deserving than I.

A psychic told me that I'm also an intergalactic sex symbol—gray, glob-like sentients on the planet Xenx saw a feature about me on *E.T. Tonight* and they, too, now lust after me.

I'm beginning to tire of all this attention. Will it never end?

Despite a jet-setting life of glamour and excitement, I'm just an ordinary guy (except that I don't fart or have body odor). I enjoy hanging out and drinking a few brewskis, as well as movies and quiet walks on the beach. So you don't need to adulate me unless, of course, you want to, in which case I won't mind at all, but I'd rather you just sent money and expensive gifts.

I was once too sexy for my shirt. I finally solved that problem—I purchased a new shirt.

I'm now officially a faery: I made a curtain for the first time. I didn't *sew* it, though; I just used iron-on tape, so I wasn't sure it counted. I was going to look up the rules in the *Faery Handbook*, but the next day, a friend visited and did a Tarot reading for me. She said, "I've never seen so many Wands!" Making the curtain worked.

I had a wonderful Christmas. Santa stopped by after he finished his deliveries to bring me an extra-special gift. The Easter Bunny may be cuter, but Santa is kinkier—he definitely knows naughty from nice. He was hot and sweaty after a hard night's work, covered in soot from all those dirty chimneys (people are so inconsiderate). We took a long bubble bath together, sipping flutes of milk and eating cookies. Then, I made him ho! ho! ho! like he'd never ho! ho! ho!'d before.

Someone I was attracted to said, "You seem more like a brother to me." So I asked, "How do you feel about incest?"

I like to state my endowment in metric—we live in a global economy, after all, plus it sounds better. Mine is thirty-one kilometers.

I am often tongue-in-check. I would prefer to have my tongue in someone else's cheek, but you can't have everything.

Okay, I didn't sleep with Santa. In fact, I'm just hoping to lose my virginity before I lose my teeth. I'm so hard up for sex that I started flying again so I could go through security and be groped. What's amazing is that, unlike checked luggage, they don't charge extra for it.

On the other hand, my alternate realities are such hotbeds of sex that it's exhausting. It's probably a good thing I'm getting such a nice rest over here. Still, like many of us, I seek my soul mate.

MY PERSONAL AD

Lemurian male, 177 cm, 90.9 kg., enjoys dancing on ceiling and wearing socks, seeking same. Cutie patootie bootie with big heart, liver, and other organs to the front of the line! Must like astral travel to other star systems. No fatties, freaks, flakes, or scales. Let's spend our next seven lifetimes together!

Dead is the new 90.

Some of my best friends are dead people.
Enlightened ones have always seen death
as just a transition, like birth.

Most people understand
that they shouldn't discriminate against others
because of the color of their skin.
Now, it's time to learn not to discriminate
against those who don't have skin.

Chapter 44

OBITUARIES

A friend told me about some rich people she knew who are on the board of directors of several organizations, mostly to give themselves longer obituaries. I realized that I need to start working on mine—I don't want to leave it to my relatives—but I wondered if I could encapsulate my life and death in a couple sentences. Here are some possibilities:

• Shepherd Hoodwin died yesterday. He is survived by himself, as well as by some people who still have bodies.

• Shepherd Hoodwin's reality show was canceled yesterday. He died from alfalfa sprout poisoning and a severe chocolate deficiency.

• Shepherd Hoodwin completed what he was determined would be his final lifetime yesterday; he was 947 years old. He met his soul mate last Tuesday.

• Shepherd Hoodwin went to Heaven in a handbasket yesterday. Today, through the medium Chester Sylvester, he said he enjoyed the trip, but next time will go through the tunnel of light like everyone else.

When you become enlightened
and remember your past lives,
you discover that not all of them were glamorous.
For every time I was a big queen like Cleopatra,
I had several more modest, hardworking lifetimes
such as Napoleon.

However, all our past lives are meaningful
and helped make us who we are.

Chapter 45

ABOUT THE AUTHOR[1]

Shepherd Hoodwin has been channeling Doreen since 211 B.C.

He arrived on Earth about eighty thousand years ago in a spaceship similar to the one Superman arrived in from Krypton, only it was larger and had a home theater. He, too, was fleeing an exploding planet, his in the Sirius star system. His spaceship splashed down off the coast of Africa, where local tribes greeted him as a god. Needless to say, that first lifetime on Earth was quite pleasant, and he reincarnated into one of those tribes for his second lifetime as well.

Later, Shepherd had several lives as prominent politicians in Atlantis. After Atlantis sank (while he was away on business in Tibet), Shepherd devoted his next millennia to serious spiritual pursuits as high priests, shamans, and erotic dancers.

Shepherd's most notable past life was as Jesus's younger brother, Joe, Jr., of Nazareth (called "Little Joe"). Interestingly, he was thought of at the time as the spiritual one in the family. To quote from the recently discovered *Absene Gospels*, "Joe wenteth to temple everyday while his older brother was out with the boys in the wilderness doing God knows what. But

---

[1] Reprinted, in part, from *The Journey of Your Soul* with the generous permission of the author.

Joe idolized his brother and died tragically the summer after his Bar Mitzvah when he literally tried to walketh in his footsteps—on the water—and drowned. It was sad he kneweth not the secret of Jesus's flotation sandals, which he had made to save ferry money."

According to Doreen, in three parallel universes Joe survived and became the Messiah rather than his big brother. (Jesus instead opened J&J Construction with John the Beloved.) As the Son of God, Joe brought massive spiritual transformation to earth by putting on a musical for Pontius Pilate rather than being crucified. It was called *Joseph and the Amazing Technicolor Dream*. Judas was especially good as Jezebel (of course, women weren't allowed to perform in musicals in those days). Not even Bette Davis was able to surpass his performance. This was Judas's true calling. It gave him a constructive outlet for his millennial angst and bitchiness—he'd always been upset that Jesus loved John best.

In more recent lifetimes, Shepherd has been a pirate, several monks, and was tortured by the Inquisition ☺. He also had several lifetimes as an agricultural engineer (formerly called "peasant"). He coauthored two brilliant bestsellers, the Bible and the *Kamasutra*. In a simultaneous lifetime, he is Steve Lawrence, who popularized the song "I've Got to Be Me" and had many other hits with his lovely wife and twin flame, Edie Gormé. In addition, he is George Clooney in several parallel universes.

This lifetime is likely Shepherd's last (but not

least). As a child, he was highly verbal and started talking seven months before birth. By the time his fetus was four months old, he could do all the voices from Howdy Doody Time. He used his mother's vagina like a sock puppet, which freaked out her gynecologist. It took Dr. Bob months to figure out where the sound was coming from. He suspected demonic possession, but fortunately, Jews don't believe in that. Shepherd's grandmother knew what it was as soon as she heard about it. "Ah, the old vagina sock puppet trick! That kid will *never* shut up." And so it was.

Although he was precocious verbally, he wasn't so much in other ways. For instance, he didn't start to walk until he was thirty-five, and that was only because the remote broke.

Shepherd is well known to many who know him. He is the author of the thriller *Burn Before Reading* and the horror classic *Survival of the Deadest*. He has a starring role on *The Real Housewives of North Las Vegas* and makes frequent appearances in male strip clubs around the country as "Flabio." He is a certified Out-of-Body Pilate™ instructor at his local Belly Total Fitness. He is also a professor emeritus at California's Hunks State University at Malibu; his published papers include "Why Long, Dangly Earrings Make the Wrong Statement" and "Tattoos: How to Choose the Right Skull and Crossbones for Your Build." He is the lead singer for Bleeding Eardrums, and wrote the country hit "Factory Farm Cowboy." He has naturally curly red hair.

His celebrity has benefited from the backlash against musclemen. People now fantasize about men like Shepherd, who perfectly epitomizes the new ideal—he has absolutely no muscles. Despite the high price of fame (including having his expensive clothes ripped off whenever he leaves the house), he takes his responsibility to humanity seriously.

Shepherd has also achieved distinction for his numerous artistic accomplishments. He is the only person ever to win the grand slam of awards: the Nobel, Oscar, Pulitzer, and Emmy (known as the NOPE). Of course, that was in a parallel universe. In this universe, he hasn't gotten much done yet, but he intends to soon.

In this universe, Shepherd was born in 1954, but everyone guesses him to be fifty-seven. He attributes his youthful good looks to clean, healthy living and stunted emotional development. Several astrologers have predicted that he would write musicals, since he's got the sun in the morning and the moon at night.

Shepherd makes his home in Laguna Niguel, California, with his significant other, Leroy, who happens to be a plant. Known as the "Doreen Channel to the Stars," Shepherd has channeled internationally, from Santa Ana to Burbank, for celebrities such as Eartha Quake, Helena Handbasket, Bing Cherry, Terra Firma, Rock Hardy, and Buck Naked.

Shepherd Hoodwin has met Shirley MacLaine's dentist.

I have been prolific lately.
(When you're enlightened,
inspiration pours through you 24/7.)
I have several exciting new books
coming out next year.

Wind has long been a symbol of spirit,
and trees represent the connection
between heaven and earth.
For that reason,
I chose for my new publishing house
the uplifting name "Breaking Wind Press."

Here are the covers, with a few excerpts:

UPCOMING TITLES

from

BREAKING WIND PRESS

THE ULTIMATE IN NEW AGE BOOKS

SPRING 2012 SEASON

HEALTH

&

NUTRITION

DIET FOR A SMALL STOMACH

Shepherd Hoodwin

FROM THE BOOK:

Chapter 3—Whole Foods

Always eat whole, unrefined foods. For example, maple syrup is a highly refined product. First, the sap is extracted from a tree. Then, it is boiled for hours, cooking out essential vitamins and enzymes. It is better to eat the whole maple tree. (See also Chapter 34, "Getting More Fiber.")

Runaway **New York Times** *Bestseller!*

THE RICESCREAM™

DIET

FOR A NEW PLANET

Shepherd Hoodwin

*A REVOLUTIONARY APPROACH
TO ELIMINATING STARVATION
& SAVING THE EARTH!*

MUSCLE TESTING
FOR
EVERYONE!

DR. SHEPHERD G. HOODWIN, Lm.NOP

A **TESTIMONIAL** FROM A SATISFIED CLIENT:

"I used to have a terrible sweet tooth. In 2010, I was 4'11" and weighed 542 lbs.

"Then, I met Dr. Hoodwin, a Certified Muscle Testing Technician. Using his patented Muscleometer, he tested my muscles and found that they were weak. He told me, 'Your belly is full, but your muscles are starving to death!' He prescribed a regimen of food supplements to nourish them back to health.

"Today, I am 6'5" and weigh 147 lbs., thanks to you, Dr. Hoodwin. You've changed my life and made this a better world."

— S.H., Laguna Niguel, CA

PSYCHOLOGY

&

SELF-HELP

MEN WHO RUN, DANCE, & DO YOGA WITH THE WOLVES

The long-awaited sequel to
Women Who Take the Bus with the Wolves

"At last, a book that shows men how to get in touch with their feelings. This is a landmark for the men's movement."
— Nancy Drewe, author of *Creeps, and the Women Who Love Them*

"This book is for sissies."
— Captain John Bly, author of *Iron Gut*

Shepherd Hoodwin

Imelda May Have
NEEDED
All Those Shoes

HOW TO LET GO OF JUDGMENT
& SHOP WITHOUT **GUILT**

Special Section
Fur—the Feel-Good Fabric

Channeled from Zsa Zsa

Shepherd Hoodwin

POTTY TRAINING YOUR INNER CHILD

DVD & WORKBOOK SET

From the Internationally Acclaimed Workshop

Shepherd Hoodwin

ONLY $89.95!

OVER $700 OFF THE WORKSHOP PRICE!

Self-Confidence

FOR

TOTAL LOSERS

Personal Growth
for the Rest of Us!

SHEPHERD HOODWIN

AUTHOR OF:

Astrophysics for Abject Morons

The Complete Guide to Dating for Smelly People

*Overcoming Your Addiction to Self-Help Books
in 39 Easy Steps*

200

How to Be a FUN HUN!

The Complete Guide to Rape and Plunder

CHANNELED FROM ATTILA

SHEPHERD HOODWIN

ROMANCE

ℵAKED SOULS

A NOVEL

A Story of Lust & Karma

"They saw each other across a crowded universe.
Their eyes met. Actually, they didn't have eyes;
they were souls—souls don't have eyeballs.
But they saw each other, don't ask me how,
and knew, just knew, that they were fated
to be together once again.
And it wasn't going to be pretty."

203

METAPHYSICAL

&

SPIRITUAL

CARE OF YOUR SOUL

Shepherd Hoodwin

AT LAST, THE COMPLETE GUIDE!

EXCERPT FROM THE BOOK:

1. Do not soak for more than three minutes. Do not bleach. Use cold or lukewarm water only.

Since reading and following the instructions in this book, my soul is cleaner and brighter, with no embarrassing mildew odor.
— Dr. Elisabeth Dübler-Einelublenherrspecktenhausen

THE BIBLE

HOODWIN VERSION

ABOUT THE AUTHOR:

GOD is the Creator of the Universe. He is most famous for parting the Red Sea in 1744 B.C. and for miracles He did with his Son and business partner, Jesus, from 24–27 A.D. God, who is also known as the Lord, Jehovah, Allah, Yahweh, and the Boys Upstairs, has received many prestigious theological awards, including being made the honorary head of several major religions. He is also a gifted artist and musician, being responsible for composing the celebrated Music of the Spheres and painting the Grand Canyon. His floral designs have won countless awards. (Yes, He is a little gay.)

God wishes to acknowledge the support He received in writing this Book from countless people, especially the Prophets, without whom He could never have written it. He is also indebted to Priscilla of Ur, who painstakingly recopied the often-illegible transcriptions of His transmissions, and to the Church Fathers, who expertly corrected spelling, punctuation, and content.

CHOOSING YOUR PARENTS

The *OFFICIAL* ASTRAL PLANE Guide

Channeled from Freddy Bob

Shepherd Hoodwin

DO-IT-YOURSELF NEAR-DEATH EXPERIENCES

How to Die & Come Back to Life

IN TEN EASY STEPS!

With **free** DVD & CosmoGlasses™

Shepherd Hoodwin

RIGHT USE
OF BILL

Channeled from God's
Nephew Seymour

Shepherd Hoodwin

With an Introduction by God

REMEMBER
BE HERE
YESTERDAY

BE HERE YESTERDAY HERE BE YESTERDAY YESTERDAY HERE BE

SPIRITUALITY FOR
TYPE A PERSONALITIES

SHEPHERD HOODWIN

SEX ON THE
ASTRAL PLANE

DEAD MOVIE STARS
TELL ALL!

With an Introduction by
MARILYN MONROE

*Those reports about me appearing
to people all over the world are false!
I'm too busy getting laid on the Astral Plane!*
— Elvis Presley

Shepherd Hoodwin

BIOGRAPHY

THE THRILLING FOURTH VOLUME OF MEMOIRS
BY AMERICA'S MOST BELOVED AUTHOR

MEN ARE FROM MARS, SHEPHERD IS FROM NEPTUNE

SHEPHERD HOODWIN

Author of the Bestsellers

LIFE IN THE RIGHT-TURN-ONLY LANE

I'M ANNOYING

SMACKED ON THE HEAD

BY THE LIGHT!

Volume V Coming Soon:

STILL NOT DEAD

Afterword

By God

LET THERE BE LIGHT ALREADY!

AUTHOR'S NOTE: It's an incredible honor to have God write the Afterword for this book. I am a *huge* fan. He is my favorite deity (after Stephen Sondheim). I've been following Him on Twitter since the Beginning. He taught me everything I know.

> *"And God said, Let there be light: and there was light.*
> *And God saw the light, that it was good:*
> *and God divided the light from the darkness.*
> *And God called the light Day,*
> *and the darkness he called Night.*
> *And the evening and the morning were the first day."*
> — *Genesis*

First of all, let Me say that I don't think anyone who would read this book is a nitwit, although it's a cute title. A nitwit cannot laugh at the foibles of life, especially his own. Believe Me, if I didn't have a sense of humor about MySelf, I wouldn't still be here. Laughter is My best creation, along with dogs (which, of course, are Me spelled backward).

I'm thrilled that the publisher asked Me to write the Afterword. For one thing, it's always a pleasure to have the last Word. When you were younger, I needed to lay down the Law sometimes so you would feel secure, and maybe I occasionally went a little overboard. There weren't any good parenting books back then. (I still think I was right about the golden calf.) In any case, now that you're older, I wait to be invited, and I do have some things to say about enlightenment.

The quote above describes what happened at the Beginning of what was, for Me, a very busy week. But what people don't understand is that every beginning is the same: Light is the beginning, not the end.

The end of that particular week culminated with My making human beings. Then I took a day off. Resting is the connective tissue between what was and what is to come, a time of absorbing what you did and preparing for what's next. Then, however, a new week came again, as it always does. The next cycle, building on what went before, always starts with light.

The common picture is that you work extremely hard, get enlightened, and then what? Twiddle your thumbs? Beam beatifically for the rest of eternity? That would be boring. No! Become enlightened, and you're just getting started.

Incidentally, "twiddle" is an excellent word that could be used more often, in a variety of contexts. Just a suggestion, not a Commandment.

Humanity isn't created once, but over and over, at new levels. By the same token, you don't become enlightened once, but have a chance to do it at a new level every week (of whatever length).

215

What does it mean to be enlightened? It's simply letting your light shine without obstruction, each time to a greater brightness because you have more awareness. A higher consciousness, like taller windows, lets in more light. With more light, you can see more of life, and live with more love. Then you get more consciousness. Rinse and repeat.

Becoming enlightened requires a willingness to let go of everything that gets in the way of who you are. That's the hard part, because much of it masquerades as protection. Maybe it was at one time. However, as you approach enlightenment, you let it go, because all you need is love (along with some street smarts). You basically just have to say, "Let there be light" and mean it.

What does enlightenment look like? For one thing, it's lighthearted; it's full of joy. Most children are enlightened, but since, by definition, they're not mature, external influences can easily distract them. Mature enlightenment is the ability to be joyful no matter what.

What does an enlightened being do? Whatever needs to be done. If the trash needs to be taken out, you take it out with music in your heart and a bounce in your step.

What comes after enlightenment? There's a whole world in need of healing, a planet that has been suffering terribly under the abuse of those who mostly don't know better. As Genesis says, the first day doesn't just involve letting there be light, but dividing it from darkness—very important. When light and darkness aren't divided, people can't tell them apart.

Those who are enlightened can educate, but knowledge alone is not enough. It's more important to help others open to their own light and experience the clarity of dividing the light from the darkness in themselves.

There's nothing wrong with darkness—I created that, too. When it's properly divided from light, it becomes Night, the time you dream and create new possibilities, when your body is re-energized so it can be ready for the activities of the Day. An increase in divine light increases divine darkness (creative possibilities). It's only a problem when light and darkness are twiddled together.

Becoming enlightened doesn't mean that you're suddenly a know-it-all. No one likes a know-it-all anyway. Even I don't know it all, although I know a lot. We each have to stay open, because none of us know exactly what the next creation will be. For example, who knew that humanity would create microwave popcorn? It never entered My Mind! I'm not saying it was such a good idea, but you never know.

I can't do it all MySelf, so get enlightened already, and let's find out together what comes next.

Will you be perfect when you're enlightened? No. And yes. As with every parent, I think my children are already perfect—you can do no wrong, as far as I'm concerned. But will you be completely free of blind spots and shortcomings? That would put us out of business—there would be nothing left to learn. Fortunately, at the end of the day, you see that it's all good.

Thank God it's now! And next week: still more enlightenment. I can hardly wait!

God
Now, Here

Epilogue

Congratulations! You have reached enlightenment (assuming you didn't skip any chapters). Enjoy! What's your next step?

Once the Mayan calendar ends in 2012, you're going to need a new one. Being here and now is great, but even enlightened people sometimes find it useful to know more specifically where they are on the space/time continuum. For that reason, we're publishing the NEW Mayan Calendar for 2013, with a pearl of wisdom for each day. Watch for it at http://enlightenmentfornitwits.com.

More Acknowledgments

Writing a book is a spiritual journey,
often traveling coach next to a fat person.
I am grateful to all those who gave me feedback,
showing me what I couldn't see and helping bring clarity
to what I was sensing but hadn't articulated.

Special thanks to Stan Grindstaff for his exquisite editing,
and (listed in reverse alphabetical order by first name):
Tina Wong, Susannah Redelfs, Renee Mumford, the MT List,
Gloria Constantin, Geoffrey Roth, Dave Gregg, & Alexandra Marx.
To each of you, I bequeath my first-born child.
Thanks also to Melody Cassen, who designed the luscious cover.

ABOUT THE AUTHOR—REALLY

SHEPHERD HOODWIN has been channeling since 1986. He also does intuitive readings, mediumship, past-life regression, healing, counseling, and channeling coaching (teaching others to channel). He has conducted workshops on the Michael teachings throughout the United States.

Watch for his hilarious audiobook of *Enlightenment for Nitwits, the NEW Mayan Calendar* for 2013, and other heavenly treats at http://enlightenmentfornitwits.com, where you can also sign up for an email list.

Upcoming books include *Opening to Healing Energy, Growing Through Joy,* and *Being in the World,* each channeled from Michael. Look for these and Shepherd's current books (listed next page) at http://summerjoy.com and popular ebook sellers.

Shepherd is also working on a follow-up to his book on the Michael teachings, *The Journey of Your Soul,* and a collection of spiritual and personal growth writings, tentatively entitled *Divine Innervention: How God Stops the Bad Guys Without Ruining Her Hair.*

Shepherd is a graduate of the University of Oregon in Music. He lives in Laguna Niguel, California.

http://summerjoy.com, enlightenmentfornitwits.com
Twitter: @EnlightenNitwit, @shepherdh
https://www.facebook.com/EnlightenmentforNitwits
sgh@summerjoy.com

Summerjoy Press
99 Pearl
Laguna Niguel CA 92677-4818

OTHER SUMMERJOY PRESS BOOKS
BY SHEPHERD HOODWIN
Available at http://summerjoy.com and soon in popular ebook formats

THE JOURNEY OF YOUR SOUL
A Channel Explores Channeling and the Michael Teachings

Journey is the most in-depth examination of the Michael teachings and the first analytical study of channeling by a channel. It has a Foreword by Jon Klimo, author of *Channeling: Investigations on Receiving Information from Paranormal Sources*. He writes, "*Journey* may well be the best (Michael book) of them all due to its clarity, thoroughness, and detail, and thanks to the fact that the author, an exceptionally clear-headed Michael channel himself, brings real integrity and authenticity." Its Appendix has the most extensive collection of Michael teachings humor anywhere (okay, the only collection).

LOVING FROM YOUR SOUL
Creating Powerful Relationships

This inspiring, transformative book is the first in the Summerjoy Michael series of books containing Michael's insights on a wide range of topics. It explores the nature of love itself as well as practical matters of relationships. It does not contain technical material about the Michael teachings but expands on many of the topics in *The Journey of Your Soul*. One reader wrote, "There are phrases that are so inspiring, I wrote them down to refer to when I need them." Next in the series are *Opening to Healing Energy, Growing Through Joy,* and *Being in the World*.

MEDITATIONS FOR SELF-DISCOVERY
Guided Journeys for Communicating with Your Inner Self

This is a beautiful collection of forty-five vivid, often pastoral, guided imagery meditations channeled from Shepherd's essence (higher self) that can be read to oneself or others. Teachers and group leaders will find it particularly useful. It includes blank pages for journaling.

ORDER FORM

ENLIGHTENMENT FOR NITWITS

Please send me (check one):

QUANTITY INVESTMENT BONUS GIFT* (& 20+ saves **40%**!)

☐ 144,000 $1,291,680   Eternal peace on earth
☐ 10,000 $89,700   Peace on earth for one month
☐ 1000 $8970   Peace in the Middle East for one week
☐ 500 $4485   Miracle healing for one fatal disease
☐ 100 $897   Miracle healing for one non-fatal disease
                           (or two rashes)
☐ 50 $448.50   Winning lotto ticket
                           (size determined by your karma)
☐ 20 $179.40   Taking care of your Christmas shopping
                           (& saving **40%**!)
☐ 10 $104.65   Making your friends ROFL
                           (& saving **30%**!)
☐ 3 $35.88   Feeling insanely happy
                           (& saving **20%**!)
☐ 1 $14.95   Becoming enlightened
                           (& getting **free shipping**!)

*Bonus gift may be delivered to an alternate universe.

☐ ____ **CUSTOM QUANTITY*** (Must be whole, positive number)
              *Quantities limited. $14.95 per book minus discount (above).

☐ Please send me, *absolutely free*, a **VIP pass into Heaven** when I die.*

*Seats at the right hand of God are available to American Express Platinum cardholders for an additional fee. Write us for details.

Prices include tax and shipping.

MAIL **CHECK** OR MONEY ORDER TO:

     Summerjoy Press
     99 Pearl,
     Laguna Niguel CA 92677-4818

TO USE **CREDIT CARD**, please go to enlightenmentfornitwits.com.